PAINLESS

Reading Comprehension

Darolyn "Lyn" Jones, Ed.D.

Third Edition

For Will, my son, whose will to live provided me the will
and inspiration to write this book.

For Jim, my husband, whose support, friendship,
and love are unconditional.

All inquiries should be addressed to:
Barron's Educational Series, Inc.
250 Wireless Boulevard
Hauppauge, New York 11788
www.barronseduc.com

ISBN: 978-1-4380-0769-4
Library of Congress Catalog Card No. 2015950148

PRINTED IN CANADA
9 8 7 6 5 4 3 2 1

CONTENTS

INTRODUCTION

This book is written for you, the student. Each of you has a toolbox in your brain. Every time you come across something that works for you, you add that tool to your toolbox.

Tools for your toolbox

From experience and practice, I have learned what tools to use when I read. I know that I need some background noise like classical music. I know that I need a pen and a packet of sticky notes because I like to underline key passages and write my thoughts down on the sticky notes. I can only read about twenty pages in one sitting, so I have to break up large reading selections into smaller parts. I know that I need to go back and reread the passages I underlined and reread my reactions and try to answer my questions. My husband, on the other hand, brings a highlighter and ink pen to the text. He retires to a quiet room, prefers to read hundreds of pages at one sitting, highlights passages, and writes notes in the margins of his book. We use different tools to read. We had to learn what those tools are from failing and practicing until we got it right.

Each one of us uses a different collection of tools to do what we need to do to learn. The trick is figuring out what tools work.

In this book, I am providing you with many tools. Try them all out, and see which ones work for you! If they work, add them to your toolbox, and use them when you read.

CHAPTER ONE

Reading Attitudes and Patterns

WHAT KIND OF READER ARE YOU?

Just as two snowflakes are not alike, neither are any two readers. Reading is a very personal and individual process. For some of you, the answer to the question, "What kind of reader are you?" is simple. You aren't! You don't read. For others, the answer might be:

- You read sometimes—when you have time.
- You read when you like what you are reading.
- You love reading and read often.

Reading strengths and weaknesses

Before you jump into this book, you need to think about what kind of reader you are. You need to consider how you feel about the act of reading and what your strengths and weaknesses are. Reading is just like any other action. It's one part ability, one part attitude, and one part practice. You have to know what your strengths are, how you feel about reading, and what parts need practice. The better you get at something, the more you like it. For example, when you first learned to play soccer, you may have known how to kick the ball but not how to pass the ball during a game. Or, blocking may have come easy for you, but traveling down the field while passing at the same time might have required more practice. Once you were able to run and pass, shoot, and block, you could successfully play the whole game! The same is true for reading.

You have the ability to read, but you must practice all the required parts of the reading process to be a successful reader.

To be a successful reader, you need to know what to do before you read, what to do while you are reading, and what to do after you have finished reading. Only you know what you can and can't do. I always tell my students that I don't have the ability to morph into Plankton and jump into their brains to find out what kind of readers they are. My goal in writing this book is to help you get to the point where you can help yourself.

TYPES OF READERS

According to Kylene Beers and Barbara Samuels in their book *Into Focus: Understanding and Creating Middle School Readers*, there are two types of readers: avid and reluctant. Someone who is **avid** at something does it often because he or she likes to. For example, most of my students admit they are avid users of Facebook, Instragram, and Snapchat. Avid readers like to read and read often. Avid readers read not because they have to but because they like to. That doesn't mean an avid reader loves everything that is read. But, an avid reader is a good reader because he or she practices![1]

Then there is the **reluctant** reader. The reluctant reader is the most complex and difficult to define. If someone is reluctant to do something, it may be because he or she doesn't want to, doesn't like to, or simply can't. For example, someone may be a reluctant dancer because she doesn't like to dance. She can dance if she has to, but she would rather be playing basketball or video games. Someone may be a reluctant tennis player because he hasn't had enough practice, isn't skilled enough at the game, and doesn't want to look foolish. Someone may be a reluctant swimmer because she can't swim and doesn't want to drown!

Step 1: What kind of reader are you?

Take some time to think about the answers to the following questions. First, decide if you are an avid or reluctant reader; then, answer the questions below!

Do you like to read? Would you say you are an avid reader? Why? What do you like to read? For example, do you read science fiction, fantasy, graphic novels, poetry, historical fiction, contemporary fiction, series books like Suzanne Collins' *Hunger Games*, or the Divergent book series, magazines like *Sports Illustrated*, popular blog posts on Tumblr, or online social news from BuzzFeed? How many books do you read in a week or a month? Why do you like reading? Is it because it is an escape or because you learn new things or a combination of factors? Do you read every chance you get, like in class and at home or just when you have total free time? Does reading come pretty easy for you? Even avid readers don't like everything they read. What do you *not* like to read and why?

If you are a reluctant reader and you don't want to read, is it because you don't like to read or because you have trouble reading, or is it a combination of both? Are there some things that you don't like to read? Why don't you like to read them? Do you have problems understanding some things when you read them? Why? Explain what gets in the way of understanding what you read.

Step 2: Check your attitude!

Now that you have identified what kind of reader you are, how do you think you got there? How did you become avid or reluctant? The following questions will help you recall your reading history and your attitude about reading. Write down your answers to the questions below:

Think of two reading memories.

- Everyone was read to when they were younger, either at home or in early elementary school. Tell me about your favorite story or a favorite person who read to you.
- Now, think about when you were in grade 3, 4, or 5 and you were expected to read more on your own. Was reading easy or harder?
- What made it easy? What made it harder? Was the reading interesting or boring? Did you like reading more than you do now? Why or why not?

Step 3: How do you read? When you read, are you alert and awake, napping, or drooling?

- When you read, are you alert? In other words, do you know and understand completely what you read the first time you read it and every time you read?
- When you read, are you awake? In other words, when you read something and are confused, do you know there is a problem so you back up and fix it and figure it out?
- When you read, do you nap? In other words, when you read something and are confused, do you know you don't get it but you don't know how to fix it?

- When you read, do you drool? In other words, when you read and are confused, do you just keep reading and have no idea what you have read?

Probably you read all these ways. You may start out bright-eyed and bushy-tailed, then you are just awake, then your head gets heavy and you nap, and finally there is a pool of drool on your book. It may also depend on what you are reading. If you are reading about your favorite basketball player, then you may be alert. If you are reading something you don't like, you may be drooling. When you are reading, you need to be aware of when you are alert and awake, napping, and drooling.

To be a successful reader and understand what you are reading, you need to be awake and alert. You need to keep what you read in your head!

If you nap or drool while you practice reading, you won't improve your reading skills. The same is true for anything you practice. If you nap or drool through your piano lessons or karate lessons, you won't get any better at playing or kicking.

BECOMING A BETTER READER

How can you make reading easier and more enjoyable?

- Know what kind of reader you are and what kind of reader you want to be.
- Have a positive attitude.
- Make a choice to practice.
- Set goals for yourself.

In the words of one of my favorite principals, Dr. Beresford, "The choices you make today shape your world tomorrow." Attitude and choice are as important as skill. Attitude is the first step to becoming a better reader, and practice is the second step. You have to make a choice to become a better reader and set the bar high; then you need to practice to reach your goal. In the movie *Rudy*, the true story of Rudy Ruettiger and his dream of playing Notre Dame football is told. He was not smart enough to get into Notre Dame, and he was too small to play football for Notre Dame. Instead of giving up on what he wanted, he decided he would do anything to reach his goal and made a choice to practice. He studied so he could first get into Notre Dame as a student; then he practiced the game of football so he could make the team as a walk on.

Here are some final thoughts for you to consider:

- Writers write about what they love and know, and they write for you, the reader.
- Readers write as much of the story as a writer does by reading and responding to the story. It takes both of you to tell the story. Reading is reciprocal.

- If you have had trouble with reading in the past, identify what kind of reader you are and think about how you got there.
- Use this book and the strategies it offers and learn to become a better reader with patience and practice.

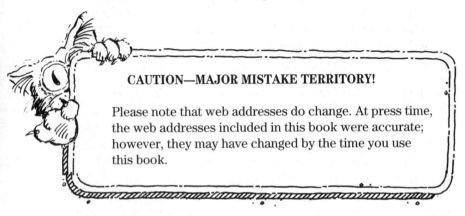

CAUTION—MAJOR MISTAKE TERRITORY!

Please note that web addresses do change. At press time, the web addresses included in this book were accurate; however, they may have changed by the time you use this book.

Surfing the web

If you go to any of the web addresses listed in this book and discover that it is no longer valid, either because the web address has changed or has been discontinued, don't worry. Simply go to your preferred search engine (mine is *Google*), and type in a key word search on the topic you are interested in. For example, if you are looking for one of the teen read sites, just type in "top teen reads." You will find many sites that discuss good books to read if you are a teen. When you do a key word search, be as specific and simple as possible. For example, if you want to find reading guides to use while you read, simply type in "reading guides." Don't type in "reading guides during reading." That's too much information.

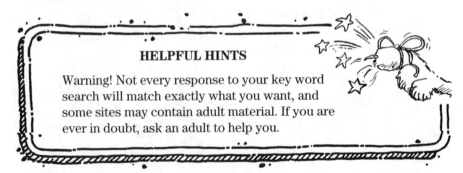

HELPFUL HINTS

Warning! Not every response to your key word search will match exactly what you want, and some sites may contain adult material. If you are ever in doubt, ask an adult to help you.

CHAPTER TWO

Preparations for Reading

WHAT SHOULD I DO BEFORE
I START READING?

There is an old saying, "If you fail to plan, you plan to fail." What does that mean? The more you do ahead of time to prepare, the easier the task will be. The more you do before you start reading, the easier reading will be.

Think about this. When a famous singer like Taylor Swift is about to perform for thousands of fans, she doesn't just run onto the stage directly from her tour bus and begin singing. She arrives at the concert venue before anyone else shows up and warms up with vocal exercises, has her hair and makeup done, gets dressed, and then runs onto the stage and begins singing. If Taylor Swift didn't do all that, her show and singing wouldn't be as good as her fans have come to expect. And because she wants success, she prepares. The same is true for reading.

Determine, decide, and deduce

If you want to be a successful reader, you have to determine, decide, and deduce!

1. *Determine your purpose.* Why are you reading this? The teacher told me to isn't a purpose. Try again. Do you have to memorize the information for a test? Do you have to summarize or retell what you read? Do you have to write a report, explaining the events and motivations? Do you have to make an online poster, like Glogster, representing symbols about the topic? Do you have to act out a scene? The possibilities are endless. If you aren't sure, then reread the assignment sheet or ask your teacher to clarify. To complete the assignment and be a successful reader, you must understand why you are reading what you have been assigned to read.
2. *Decide what kind of material you are reading.* Is it informational—just facts and dates? Is it fiction—a story? Is it a word problem you will have to solve? Is it a process—like how a piece of wood becomes a fossil? Just as we speak in different "languages" in different situations, we read differently depending on what we are reading.

3. *Deduce how much time you will need to do the reading.*
Deduce or make an educated guess as to how long you will
need to do the reading, and then add some extra time to that.
Have you ever tried to read a fifteen-page chapter in study
hall thirty minutes before it is due? Were you successful?
Probably not. Give yourself plenty of time. Some people
need longer than others, and that is okay. You won't be given
an award for speed reading. People who say they can read
really fast may be able to, but they may also just be saying
the words and not reading. You know the difference so don't
feel pressured to read faster. The reward for slowing down
is that you understand what you have read. Only you know
how long it takes you. So, set aside that amount of time
and some extra time in case you run into problems. In the
Introduction, I shared with you that I can read only about
twenty pages at a time. When I have a lot of reading due, I
read a little, take a break and work on something else like
answering emails or checking my Facebook page, and then
come back and read more until the reading is completed. As
you read more and practice the techniques in this book, you
will discover that you will be able to read faster. But, remember, reading is a process. You need to start at the beginning
with these three steps.

- First, determine your purpose. Why are you reading this?
- Second, decide. Are you going to be reading fiction (a
  story) or nonfiction (like a textbook chapter or an article)?
- And finally, deduce. How long do you think it will take
  you to do the reading? Schedule time to read just like
  you schedule your sports, music, or karate practices and
  lessons!

Let's Practice!

*Try this exercise. Imagine you just received your driver's
license.*

*You take your dad's car out for the first time, and you take
your eyes off the road for just a second and hit the car in front
of you. No one is hurt, but both cars are damaged. Write down*

or type what you would say or how you would describe the accident to

- *the police*
- *your parents*
- *your best friend (text your best friend)*

The descriptions are very different, aren't they? Your description to the police would read as an information piece because that is all they want to know: who, what, where, and how fast. Your description to your parents might have some fiction blended in with the facts in the hopes you won't get in as much trouble. You may not tell them that you were concentrating on the car stereo and not on the road. Your description to your best friend might be an even more dramatic account, giving greater details about what you were really doing and how it felt when you hit the car and had to tell your dad. (Just so you know, your parents will find out the truth. It's better to be honest ahead of time.) Reading material also presents itself in different "languages." By deciding ahead of time what kind of reading it is, you can prepare your reading brain to make sense of the words.

Let's Practice!

An English and social studies selection about Holocaust survivor, Agnes Vogel, appears at the end of this chapter. Read about the required assignment before you read about Mrs. Vogel's life.

Your Assignment: The excerpt on page 20 is a biography written about Holocaust survivor, Agnes Vogel. Your assignment after you read the biography is to write down or type a summary of the biography pointing out three facts about the Holocaust and three places Agnes traveled on her journey of survival.

Determine

First, *determine*. What is your purpose for reading this selection?

ANSWER: To write or type a summary discussing three facts about the Holocaust and three places. So, as you read, you know to look for or focus on those facts and reasons while you are reading.

Decide

Second, *decide*. What kind of reading is it?

ANSWER: Well, you know it is written about someone's life, which makes it true. So, it is nonfiction or more specifically a biography. You also know the passage is about someone who survived something from the past. From those two facts, you should realize this won't be a story with plot and characters but rather a true story with real events, facts, and insights into how it felt to live through something so horrific as the Holocaust.

Deduce

Third, *deduce*. How long will it take you to read this?

ANSWER: How long does it normally take you to read two pages? Do you normally read stories or fiction faster than nonfiction? Most people read fiction faster. So, give yourself some extra time.

READING ORGANIZERS

Reading organizers can help you even before you start reading.

Reading organizers are just what they sound like. They help you organize your reading. Reading organizers show your thinking on paper. They can help you even before you start to read!

Reading organizers are like glue. They help your brain stick to the reading. Now, there are three main types of glue: Elmer's, Rubber Cement, and Superglue. Elmer's will hold for a while,

Rubber Cement will hold longer, and Superglue can hold forever. I want what you read to stick to your brain like Superglue!

Before you read, reading organizers can remind you of what you already know about a topic and help you to think about what you want or need to know about a topic. Reading organizers ask you to use your background knowledge. Anytime you can connect or glue yourself to what you are reading, the easier and more interesting the reading will be.

Background knowledge can include what you learned from your family and friends, in another class at school, from the media, online, or from other books.

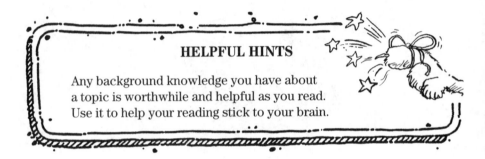

HELPFUL HINTS

Any background knowledge you have about a topic is worthwhile and helpful as you read. Use it to help your reading stick to your brain.

The anticipation guide

A terrific reading organizer to use before reading is an Anticipation Guide. If you anticipate something, then you look forward to it, or you have an expectation or idea about something. For example, most of us anticipate a vacation on the beach. We have certain expectations or ideas about how our vacation will be. An Anticipation Guide is a super way to begin thinking about your reading topic before you read. An Anticipation Guide asks you what you already know for sure about a topic and what you think you know about a topic. Then, after you read, you can see how correct your anticipations were. My Anticipation Guide is adapted from Richard and Jo Anne Vacca's book, *Content Area Reading: Literacy and Learning Across the Curriculum*.[2]

The KWL chart

Another helpful graphic organizer to use before you read is a
KWL Chart, which was created by Donna Ogle. A **KWL Chart**
stands for what you *know*, what you *want* to know, and what
you *learned*.[3] When filling out this chart you don't have to write
in complete sentences. You can just jot down words or phrases
that come to mind when considering the topic. Only the "what
you *know*" and "what do you *want* to know" columns are completed before you read.

Eye think guide

A third reading organizer is the
Eye Think Guide. When you look at
the reading passage, what do you see?
What do you think? Picture and predict.
For example, look at the pictures and
illustrations. Most reading selections will include pictures,
graphics, or figures that give you hints about what you are going
to read.

HELPFUL HINTS

Remember, fiction is not true, and nonfiction
is true.

If there are pictures, stop and look. Look at the cover of the
book. Look at the art on the page with the short story. Look at
the diagram in the science chapter. Look at the map in the social
studies selection. Look at the title. First, ask yourself how you
know it is the title. Sometimes, the title is centered at the top of
the passage or it is in all capital letters or it is in italics or it has
quotation marks around it. Does the title have a subtitle that
appears after the title? What extra information does it provide
about the title and what you will be reading? Look at the headings and the words in boldfaced type and/or italics. What hints
do they offer about the reading?

Let's Practice!

Before you read about Agnes Vogel, who survived the Holocaust during World War II, use the Anticipation Guide, KWL Chart, and Eye Think Guide to anticipate and think about what you know about the Holocaust and World War II.

HOLOCAUST ANTICIPATION GUIDE

Read each statement carefully and decide whether you agree or disagree with each statement. On a separate sheet of paper or on your computer write or type two or three sentences explaining your decision.

Jews were the only victims of the Holocaust.

The persecution of the Jews was the cause of World War II.

Adolf Hitler believed that people of northern European descent were superior to other ethnic groups.

Nobody helped the Jews of Europe escape from the Nazis.

Only Americans helped to liberate the concentration camps at the end of World War II.

The Holocaust could never happen again.

HOLOCAUST KWL CHART

Before you read the biography about Holocaust survivor Agnes Vogel, complete the KWL Chart that follows and complete the K column and the W column. What do you *know* about the Holocaust and World War II? What do you *want* to know?

K	W	L

Don't read about Mrs. Vogel yet. After you complete the KWL Chart, you should complete the Eye Think Guide. You don't have to complete three before-reading activities, but we are just practicing different ones so you can see what tool works best for you!

HOLOCAUST EYE THINK GUIDE
Picture and predict before you read!

What do you see in the pictures? Write down or type a description of the pictures. Can you guess what you might be reading about based on what you see in the pictures?

Read the title. What picture do you see in your mind when you see the words in the title and subtitle? What else do you think you will learn from this reading passage?

What do you picture when you read those heading titles? Write down or type a description of what you visualize. Can you predict what else you might be learning as you read?

HELPFUL HINTS

What do other teens do before they read?
Teens who have been successful readers in English classes share the following strategies with you!

- Before you start to read, make sure that you have bright lights on and are in a quiet place, and play music that you won't sing along with!

- Don't be freaked out by the number of pages you have to read. Divide what you have to read into shorter sections and read one section at a time. Put an M & M after every page to encourage you to keep reading!

- Before you start, think about what you already know about the topic.

- Read a little, stop and do some of the assignment, and then read some more. It's less boring that way because you do some reading and some writing.

English and Social Studies Selection:
"Agnes Vogel: Survivor from Hungary" by Kelly Watson

Agnes Vogel's story of survival during the Holocaust is one of indescribable courage. A long-time resident of Indianapolis, Indiana, Agnes and her late husband Michael Vogel were outspoken voices of the Holocaust for Indiana school children, speaking all over the state about the dangers of hate and the lessons of the Holocaust. Mrs. Vogel was interviewed by an eighth grade student and Mrs. Watson as part of a project for the United States Holocaust Memorial Museum.

Agnes's Early and Happy Life

On January 21, Martin Luther King Jr. Day, a day when the world remembers a man who fought for liberty, justice, and freedom for all, I talked to a woman who was robbed of all those things and thrown into the open jaws of the Holocaust so many years ago.

Agnes Veronica Wieisz was born in Debrecen, Hungary, in the 1930s. She has faint memories of growing up with a big backyard and going to birthday parties and movies with her friends on rainy afternoons. She grew up as the oldest of four girls. Her father worked as a representative for a farming machinery company. Overall, Agnes had a very normal childhood. That was all about to change.

War, Persecution, and the Ghetto

On March 19, 1944, at her home in Debrecen, Agnes recalls watching enormous black planes fly across the dark, cloudy sky. The German planes landed in the city, and the next morning German soldiers roamed everywhere.

From that point on Agnes remembers everything in fast forward. On April 5, she was told to wear a yellow star, and one month later on May 6, 18-year-old Agnes was taken to the ghetto in the heart of the city.

In the beginning of June an air raid struck the city. A voice on a loudspeaker informed all Jews to be out by afternoon; the Nazis were liquidating the ghetto. Agnes and her family followed the orders, although they had no idea where they were going next. In the afternoon, two men and one woman made their way through the city, checking to make sure no person took anything of value out. Agnes remembers the woman taking her mother into the back room and physically feeling her over to ensure nothing was smuggled out. Finally, they boarded trains. They were on the trains all night, but the trains did not move. The cattle cars were cramped, hot, and dark.

After a night of mental torture—knowing where they were headed, but not sure why they were stopped—the cars started to move. After looking out the small cracks in the transport cars, everyone was surprised to find that they were going toward Budapest. They headed onward until they realized they were in Austria. In the small town of Strasoff, between the Hungarian border and Vienna, their cars stopped once more.

The Concentration Camp

In Strasoff there was a camp that had not been used. They unloaded and immediately formed two groups: women on one side, men on the other. Agnes followed her mother and sisters into a very large room, big enough for hundreds. They were told to get completely naked, and a German doctor came in to inspect them all. Agnes was wearing a delicate silver chain with the Star of David on it around her neck. When the young doctor reached her, he tore the necklace off her neck and stuffed it in

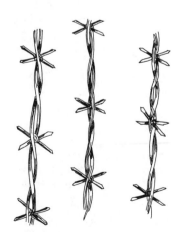

his pocket. He proceeded to go on, but a woman behind Agnes said
something to him in German. She has vivid memories of the woman
who so bravely stood up for her rolling around on the floor in pain
after a hard kick in the back from the insulted doctor.

Again they were put back on the cattle cars and taken to the
industrial part of Vienna. They stayed in a school, and her father
soon went to work at a factory. While Agnes and other young
women her age went to work at a housing project every day, her
mother and young sisters stayed at the school where they lived.
The girls mixed mortar and cleaned brick for days upon days. There
were terrifying air raids three to four times a day, but one in particular stands out in Agnes's mind. It was a bright, sunny afternoon,
and there was not a cloud in the crystal blue sky. Agnes saw a plane
was hit and watched as a man in a bright white parachute floated
to the ground. She still claims today it was the most beautiful
thing she ever saw in her life.

The Death Camp: Bergen-Belsen

After almost eleven months of tedious work and unbearable living
conditions, they were taken back to Strasoff for reasons unknown
to them. Strasoff was in a terrible condition, and there was no
food. After a terrible but short time there, they loaded the cattle
cars for one of the few remaining times, supposedly headed for
the labor camp Bergen-Belsen. As they sat in the cars, ready to
leave, an air raid began. Agnes recalls the unmistakable noise that
a bomb makes as it falls to the ground. She smiles as she explains
the way her father would stretch his arms around the whole family
each time the whistle of a bomb drew near.

Amazingly, not one of the twenty-five cattle cars was damaged
from the vicious bombings. After that, they were let out of the cars
and the conditions became considerably better. They had no way to
clean themselves, so the hygiene worsened, but there was enough
food for a while. However, lice were everywhere and hope seemed to
be running out.

Liberation

On April 10, 1945, sounds of fighting could be heard from all
directions. The Russians were coming from the east, and the
Americans from the west. Agnes laughs as she imagines the
Germans who had guarded her that same day, crawling like babies,
running away from Vienna.

The very next morning the Russians marched into camp. Agnes shudders as she explains a terrifying time. That afternoon some Russian soldiers began gathering up young girls to "go peel potatoes in the kitchen." Agnes's mother and two aunts would not let Agnes out of their sight, so luckily she was spared the nightmare that many young women faced that night. Each and every one returned at midnight screaming with terror and pain because each one had been raped. It is these kinds of unthinkable things that make Agnes's liberation process a terror in her memory.

Journey Home

The prisoners stayed for only three more days and then were told to get out. They could not go west because fighting was still going on, so their only option was to go back where they came from. They gathered their last possessions and started walking east on a journey for home. As they walked, the Russians were coming in the other direction, and at one point a Russian soldier came across the road to ask Agnes's father to light his cigarette. Being a polite gentleman, he obliged and lit the soldier's cigarette. As he did so, the Russian spotted a shiny watch on her father's arm. Someone he worked with in the factory had given the watch to him. The Russian demanded he give the watch to him. Of course, Agnes's father refused. The Russian went across the road, came back with an open bayonet, and said, "Give me your watch." Agnes's father gave him the watch.

They continued on their way and stopped at the Hungarian border. They loaded cattle cars and headed back to their hometown. As they trudged into the city, looking tattered and worn, a few young men stopped them. Through their conversation the men let them know they wished the Germans had done what they intended to do. Dumbfounded and exhausted, they came to their home, only to find it completely empty.

The United States

Not long after returning home, Agnes, a grown adult, decided she could no longer live in Hungary. She quickly made plans to move to the United States of America to stay with her aunts in Detroit. There she claims she started her life. She has worked to move past the devastating tragedy that affected millions of other Jews just like her. Through it all, she has learned valuable life lessons, most of which the average person will never understand.

WARM UP FOR READING

Did completing the Anticipation Guide, part of the KWL Chart, and the Eye Think Guide help to make your reading of Mrs. Vogel's heroic tale easier? Was your reading brain warmed up? That's right—warmed up! When it's cold outside, we often go out and start our cars before we get in. Starting the car and letting it run allows the engine to warm up, which melts the snow and ice, makes the inside warm and toasty, and helps the engine and car run more efficiently. By warming up our cars, we ensure a better performance from our vehicles once we put them into drive.

How many of you warm up or stretch out before you play basketball, volleyball, soccer, or some other sport? We all do! It's important to warm up your muscles before working them hard. If you don't warm up first, you could get injured! Also, if your muscles aren't warm, you won't play as well.

The same is true for reading. If you don't warm up your reading brain to the ideas you are going to be reading about, then you may not perform as well. If you think about what you are reading before you read it, you can avoid a brain cramp and be guaranteed a smoother per- formance.

REFLECT ON WHAT YOU HAVE LEARNED!
1. Which one of the before-reading ideas worked best for you?
2. Could you warm up better with Determine, Decide, and Deduce or the Anticipation Guide?
3. Was the KWL Chart or the Eye Think Guide easier to use?
4. Which ones will you add to your toolbox and use again?
5. Why do you think they were easier for you?

BRAIN TICKLERS
Set # 1

Use the strategies you just read about to answer the following questions! You will find the answers at the end of the chapter.

1. Before you begin reading, you should:
   a. Decide whether or not you want to read the text.
   b. Determine your purpose, decide the genre, and deduce the time.
   c. Decide the audience, determine the length, and deduce the genre.
   d. Deduce the purpose and time and determine the genre.

2. Reading organizers help you to visualize your reading. Reading organizers are like:
   a. Glue because they help your brain stick to the words.
   b. Paper because they show what you think.
   c. Paintbrushes because they illustrate the words.
   d. Lines that connect the dots.

3. It is important to think about what you know about a topic before you read. A KWL Chart helps organize your thoughts before you read. What does the KWL stand for?
   a. Key, Wish, Link
   b. Know, Will, Learn
   c. Key, Went, Low
   d. Know, Want, Learn

(Answers are on page 30.)

MASTERING MULTIPLE-CHOICE QUESTIONS

At various points throughout the book, you will encounter other "Brain Ticklers," which use multiple-choice questions to quiz you over what you have learned from the reading in that section.

Answering multiple-choice questions about a reading selection can be tricky, so use the following strategies to help you master them!

Understand question design

First, you need to know how multiple-choice questions are designed. Typically there are four answer choices but only one correct answer. So you have a 25% chance of getting the answer correct if you answer every question. If you can eliminate one or two choices, your chances of getting the correct answer are improved. If, for some reason, there is a full penalty for wrong answers and you are unable to eliminate any of the choices, you should leave questions you don't know blank, as you have a 75% chance of getting that answer wrong. However, if wrong answers are penalized a fraction of a point, you might want to guess. If this information is not explained to you, ask before you answer any questions. It pays to know how tests are scored so be a smart test-taker!

Check the time

Second, you need to find out how much time you will have to answer the questions. Keep track of your time so you don't spend too many minutes on any one question.

Answer without looking at the choices

Third, you need to know how to answer multiple-choice questions successfully. Before you even look at the possible answers, read the question twice. Try to answer it in your own words. Then, see what answer best fits your answer. If you don't see exactly what you are looking for, look for what most closely matches your answer. There may be one answer that is very obviously wrong, and then there may be another answer that also may be apparently wrong. You may struggle with the final two answers. Don't argue between the two answers. Choose the one that you believe best matches the question and the text.

Move on

It's best to skip questions you don't know and return later to try to figure them out. After you have answered what you do know and if you have time, go back to the text and try to find the answer. If you don't have time, pick the one your instinct tells you is correct. After you have marked an answer, don't change it. Research shows that going with your first answer is always the best strategy.

HERE ARE SOME STRATEGIES FOR MASTERING MULTIPLE-CHOICE QUESTIONS:

- Read the question twice.
- Answer first without looking at the answers.
- Look at the answers and see if your answer is one of the four options.
  —If it is, mark it and move on.
  —If it's not, put a star or a check or some type of notation next to the question in the margin and come back to it later, if you have time.
- Answer all the questions you know the answer to first.
- When you have answered what you do know, go back to the questions you noted.
- Eliminate, even mark out if you are allowed, the answers that you know are wrong.
- Go back to the text and look for the choices that remain and choose the correct answer.
- If you can't find the answer and there is no penalty, then guess.
- Remember, go with your first idea—it's usually right.

CAUTION—MAJOR MISTAKE TERRITORY!

Most mistakes made on multiple-choice questions are caused by:

- not reading the question carefully
- not answering the question in your head first before looking for the answer
- not reading through all of the possible answers
- taking too much time on one question
- not looking for answers in the text
- changing the first answer

BRAIN TICKLERS
Set # 2

How do you successfully master multiple-choice questions?

1. If there are four possible answers to a multiple-choice question and there is no penalty for answering incorrectly, then you should
   a. Answer the question only if you know the answer.
   b. Answer the question correctly.
   c. Pick a selection that you think is best.
   d. Guess the answer.

2. When you are answering multiple-choice questions and you don't know the answer, you should
   a. Mark it and return later to answer it.
   b. Guess.
   c. Ask for help.
   d. Choose the first choice.

3. When you first encounter a multiple-choice question, you should
   a. Read the answer choices before reading the question.
   b. Mark the first choice you see that comes close to answering the question.
   c. Change your answer.
   d. Read the question twice.

(Answers are on page 30.)

BRAIN TICKLERS—THE ANSWERS

Set # 1, page 25

1. **b.** You need to know your purpose so your reading can be guided, the genre (fiction or nonfiction) so you know whether or not you will be reading fact or fiction, and how long it will take so you can plan and won't be rushed.

2. **a.** Reading organizers do help you visualize and put your thoughts on paper, but their biggest benefit is that they help you stay connected to what you are reading.

3. **d.** Remember, it is what you **know**, what you **want** to know, what you have **learned**.

Set # 2, page 28

1. **c.** Choices a and b are obviously wrong because, of course, you should do that if you can, and it has no relevancy to the question. The answer could be either choice c or d; you should guess if you don't know since there is no penalty for guessing. Choice c is best because it clarifies that you should make an effort to answer the question, because you have a 25% chance of getting the answer correct.

2. **a.** Choices c and d are obviously wrong because no one will tell you the answer and the correct answer will never be in the same position. Now, choices a and b are both correct, but choice a is the better answer because, if you have time, that is the preferred method. You may find two answers that are both correct and discussed in the reading, but you should go with the better answer, the one that provides more details such as answer choice a in this question.

3. **d.** Rereading is a very helpful technique. You should immediately know that choices b and c are wrong because they discuss answering the question, not reading the question. Choice a seems like it could work, because it is a strategy, but before you read the choices, you have to read the question.

CHAPTER THREE

Your Reading Voices

WHAT IF I DON'T UNDERSTAND WHAT I AM READING?

There are three steps in learning to read: Decoding, Fluency, and Comprehension. First, we learn to decode or turn letters into words and recognize individual words. Then, we learn to recognize and read groups of words fluently in sentences and passages. Finally, we learn to make meaning of those sentences and passages. We understand or comprehend what we have read.

Did you know that there are three types of voices that speak to you while you are reading? No, you aren't crazy! This happens to everyone. According to Cris Tovani in her book *I Read It, but I Don't Get It: Comprehension Strategies for Adolescent Readers*, you hear the following voices when you read.

- **Reciting** You hear the reciting voice when you are only "word calling" or just mouthing the words. You really don't understand what you are reading.
- **Conversation** You hear the conversation voice when you are having a conversation with what you are reading. Your conversation voice can be good or bad. If your voice is asking questions, arguing, agreeing, disagreeing, identifying, or inferring, then it's helping you read.
- **Distracting** But, if you are reading about the Boston Tea Party and start thinking about the big party you are going to on Friday night, then your conversation voice turns into the distracting voice. This voice pulls you away from what you are reading.[4]

BE A GOOD READER

Because reading is a very personal process, there is no "one size fits all" formula. You have to find the best tools to help *you*. One thing we all can do is find out what good readers do when they don't understand what they are reading. That makes sense, right? If you want to be a good basketball player, you study the pros like Stephen Curry. You need to learn what they do and try their techniques! Likewise, if you want to be a good reader, do what the avid readers do!

GOOD READERS SHARE
SIMILAR MIND-SETS.

- They have something like a video camera inside their heads as they read. When the camera shuts off and the reader can no longer get a visual image from the words, then they know that their reading has been interrupted or distracted.
- They don't let their minds wander. When they notice their minds wandering, they stop and retell or write or tell some part of what they have read and get reconnected to the reading.
- They ask questions when they don't understand something.
- They know the characters or people in the reading passage, can keep track of them, describe them, and tell about them.
- They pay attention to the voices in their head and keep the conversation voice going so they can understand what they read to keep what they read in their head![5]

Good readers also know and use many different strategies for different *types* of reading. Remember, when you are reading, you have to determine your purpose for reading, decide what you are reading, and deduce how much time you will need to complete the reading.

So, how do you do that?

- Read from front to back.
- Be selectively attentive. You don't have to read and understand every single word.
- If you know what you are reading for, you can look for words or phrases that meet that purpose.
- Make notes while you read. Write down or type important facts, events, people, ideas, or dates.
- Make sure your video camera is turned on. Create images and interpret what you are reading. Remember, words by themselves are just black marks. Words only have meaning when you assign them meaning. You are the camera person; you are in control!

Research shows that note taking and summarizing are two of the very best ways to increase academic success in any content area.

CAUTION—MAJOR MISTAKE TERRITORY!

When you are reading, don't let the camera slow down too much because your brain forgets what you have read! The faster you read, the easier it is to remember what you have read so far. When you read too slowly, your video camera doesn't have enough power to focus on the whole idea because it is only focusing on the individual word.

Listen to the voices in your head! If you are reading and find yourself only mouthing the words or thinking about what you are going to watch on television or wear to school the next day, you need to stop and have a conversation with the words: argue with the words, repeat what the words said, or respond to the words. The strategies in this book will provide you with tools and show you how to use them successfully.

USING READING ORGANIZERS

Reading organizers can help you understand what you read. Remember, reading organizers can guide you, prompt you, and help you stay connected to what you are reading—so you can keep what you read in your head!

Next, we will look at three examples of reading organizers you can use during reading: Make an Inference, Text to Self Connections, and SAM the Summarizer. Just like in Chapter Two, I will provide you with an assignment so you have a purpose for your reading.

What is an "inference," you ask?

Making inferences is one of the most important strategies to use while reading. An inference is something that is deduced from evidence in the text (much like what a detective does). **When you make an inference, you interpret or draw conclusions from what is not exactly said.** An inference is a reasoning activity. *To infer* is to reason, to deduce, or to lead to a conclusion.

CAUTION—MAJOR MISTAKE TERRITORY!

Inferences are *not* opinions. Inferences use evidence (words and phrases from what you are reading) and personal experiences. When you make an inference or infer, you are using clues from the reading and from your personal connections.

Inferences are not seen text. Seen text is anything you can see when you read—words, pictures, charts, graphs, and any visual cues that can be used to make meaning—it is what is actually on the page. Inferences are not directly stated by the author. Unseen text is the information that lives inside your head. Inferences come from inside your head. *To infer* means to read between the lines. You put together your background knowledge (what you know about a topic) with the author's clues to produce answers or solutions to what you are reading.[6]

Let's Practice!

Read the following passage and check out the student model using the reading organizer on drawing inferences. As in Chapter Two, I will provide you with an assignment to help guide your reading.

Your Assignment: Why do you think Mohandas Gandhi embraced Thoreau's ideas and acted upon those ideas as a way to challenge the governments in South Africa and India?

Social Studies Selection: "Civil Disobedience"
by Mike Fassold

Gandhi: Introduction

In protest of the United States' war with Mexico and its de facto support of slavery, Henry David Thoreau (1817–1862) wrote the pamphlet, *On the Duty of Civil Disobedience*. In it he said, "Unjust laws exist: shall we be content to obey them, or shall we endeavor to amend them, and obey them until we have succeeded, or shall we transgress them at once?" He offered a nonviolent option to the masses to stop the actions of a government. In his case, he hoped to inspire others to join him in not paying the federal government's poll tax, thereby forcing the government to fill its jails with law-breakers. The resulting financial burden of the loss of tax revenue and prisoner upkeep would force the government to end the Mexican War and take a stand against slavery. While his idea failed at the time, the concept passed to future generations that would realize the power of civil disobedience.

Gandhi: Early Influences

The most famous of all the practitioners of civil disobedience was Mohandas K. Gandhi (1869–1948). He was born in India at the height of Britain's colonial rule of its "Jewel of the Crown." Great Britain's seizure of the once powerful Asian empire brought great wealth to the colonial power and even greater suffering to the masses of India's majority.

In his youth, Gandhi embraced the ideal of the British Empire and worked to capture its power. He even rebelled against his Hindu beliefs as a teen and sought to capture the power of the British by eating meat. Gandhi adopted British dress and sought to emulate the very British that ruled his country. Gandhi left for Great Britain in his late teens to become a lawyer.

Gandhi: Defeating Discrimination

After Gandhi's completion of the bar exam, he returned to India to practice. His law practice was not successful. In order to find work, he agreed to travel to South Africa where he would serve as a legal advisor to a Muslim businessman from India. In South Africa he felt the full force of racism and discrimination in his first few days in the British colony. The South Africa government passed laws that imposed special poll taxes on workers from India, required Indians to carry travel passes when traveling, and declared that all non-Christian marriages were invalid. To combat the racism and discrimination, Gandhi decided to make the oppressor realize its injustice and inhumanity through nonviolent resistance. After 20 years in South Africa and countless nonviolent protests and actions, Gandhi was able to defeat the discriminatory legislation against Indians living in South Africa.

In 1915, Gandhi returned to India. For the next 40 years Gandhi would wage nonviolent resistance against the superior military force. In the early years, Gandhi concentrated on local struggles. . . . His success in winning battles against British landlords and local magistrates earned Gandhi a reputation for action. His voice would become a leading voice for Home Rule in India.

Gandhi: Inspiring a Nation

Gandhi would call for complete non-cooperation by Indians. Gandhi wrote: "The British have not taken India; we have given it to them. They are not in India because of their strength, but because we keep them." In early 1930, the Indian National Congress and Gandhi launched a full-scaled nonviolent resistance campaign against the British. Gandhi notified the British viceroy that they would break the "salt laws" (the British maintained a monopoly on the production of salt) in protest over the lack of progress for Indian home rule. From the middle of March to the early part of April, marchers traveled over 220 miles from Porbander to Dandi. Once the hundreds of thousands arrived at the beach, Gandhi picked up a handful of natural salt to symbolize the breaking of the law. To enforce the law the British arrested Gandhi, leaders of the Indian National Congress, and thousands involved in the breaking of the law. In order to break the campaign, the British viceroy agreed to host talks with Gandhi about independence. Even though the talks were fruitless and Gandhi was arrested again shortly after his return, the success of the campaign would inspire India to continue its path of civil disobedience.

MAKE AN INFERENCE

Choose something from the reading you did not understand. Write it down or type it as a question. Then, using word clues in the text, add any background knowledge (what you know about a topic) you can supply to make an inference. Remember, there may be more than one answer.

What is a question you have from your reading?

What is civil disobedience?

What do *you* know about this topic?

I saw part of a movie once on TV about Gandhi. I know that Gandhi was from India. I know he stood up for the poor and starved himself. My brother is in high school and he had to read Thoreau, so Thoreau must be some kind of writer.

Go back to the text and write down any actual evidence (words, phrases, or sentences) that might help you answer your question.

For example, what are Thoreau's ideas? How did Gandhi use them?

Thoreau (1817–1862) wrote the pamphlet, *On the Duty of Civil Disobedience*. He offered a nonviolent option to the masses to stop the actions of a government. Gandhi would wage nonviolent resistance against the superior military force. To combat racism and discrimination, Gandhi decided to make the oppressor realize its injustice and inhumanity through nonviolent resistance. After 20 years in South Africa and countless nonviolent protests and actions, Gandhi was able to defeat the discriminatory legislation.

Combine all the clues in the text with your background knowledge and try to answer your question, "What is civil disobedience?"

Both men used nonviolence, or civil disobedience, as a way to make changes in the government. So, civil disobedience must mean disobeying, but in a nonviolent or civil way.

Connect with the text

> **Your Assignment:** Write down or type a paragraph explaining Emily Dickinson's message to you, the reader.

Check out this student example that uses the **Text to Self Connections** reading organizer, adapted from *I Read It, but I Don't Get It*, with the Emily Dickinson poem, "I'm Nobody."

"I'm Nobody"
by Emily Dickinson

I'm nobody! Who are you?
Are you nobody too?
Then there's a pair of us—don't tell!
They'd banish us, you know.

How dreary to be somebody!
How public like a frog
To tell your name the livelong day
To an admiring bog!

TEXT TO SELF CONNECTIONS

Copy a sentence or a passage from what you are reading and then write or type the connections you made between what you wrote down—what is from the book—and your own life. Be as specific as possible.

When you read through the student model, read all the answer choices and see which one fits best.

1. When I see these words in the text:

    Then there's a pair of us—don't tell.

    The picture in my head looks like . . .
    A. Two people   B. A frog   C. A ghost

    Choice A is the best answer because "a pair" means two.

2. When I see these words in the text:

   How dreary to be somebody!

   I think they mean . . .
   A. that it's cool to be a somebody!
   B. that it's better to not be popular.
   C. that it's dark and gloomy.

   Choice B is the best answer because the author is saying that it would be a drag to be a somebody just like a dreary day outside is no fun either.

3. When I see these words in the text:

   I'm nobody! Who are you?

   I feel . . .
   A. happy because I'm proud to not be "popular."
   B. sad because sometimes I feel like a loser.
   C. Both A and B

   Choice C is the best answer because depending on your interpretation—whether or not you think being popular is cool—both answers will fit.

4. When I see these words in the text:

   Then there's a pair of us—don't tell!

   I think they are important because . . .[7]

   A. only my best friend and I should know each other's secrets.
   B. she is saying that being a nobody means you really are a somebody, and you're not alone, but you don't get bugged all the time like when you are a somebody.
   C. it's a secret—don't tell the popular people!

Choice B is the best answer. While the author, Emily Dickinson, is saying it's a secret, she is also saying that the "nobodies" really are important. And, if the nobodies tell the "somebodies" that the nobodies are important, then the somebodies may want to be just like them. It's like saying that being a nobody is one of the best kept secrets—a secret club that you don't want anyone else to be a part of!

SAM THE SUMMARIZER

A summary is a recap in your own words of what you have just read. A summary is typically short—only a few sentences or one paragraph long. Sounds easy, right? Not necessarily, because when you write a summary, you have to take the most important ideas of the author and shorten them—but the end result still has to make sense! Summary writing is very important because it shows that you know how to combine the author's ideas and your words to create something new that explains what the author is saying. And because it is so short, you have to choose your words carefully!

SAM can help you summarize. When you Summarize, first Analyze, and then Map out the most important ideas.

- **Step 1:** Analyze and decide what is important. Look at your assignment question as a guide. If the passage is short, go through each paragraph one at a time, looking for the important words, explanations, or opinions that provide information regarding the question being asked. If the passage is long, put two or three paragraphs together and again circle, write, or type words that are important. If you feel more comfortable writing in sentences and do not want to just list words or phrases, you can use prompts such as *This paragraph is mostly about . . .* or *This passage talks mainly about . . .* (again, list words, explanations, or opinions).
- **Step 2:** Map it out. When you map something out, you have to decide what the most important landmarks and features of that map will be, as well as how those features will combine to present the clearest path. The same is true when writing a summary. After you take in all of the important words, explanations, and opinions of the author, you then have to rewrite the main idea using your

own voice. When you rewrite something in your own words, you really show that you understand it, because your words always make more sense to you than someone else's. Don't worry if your sentences are short or if your language choice isn't as fancy as the author's. You aren't writing a book; you are summarizing to show that you understand what you read so you can keep it in your head!

SAM THE SUMMARIZER: EXAMPLE

Check out another student example using the social studies selection you read earlier on Civil Disobedience and the reading organizer titled SAM the Summarizer. The student has listed two possible replies for each section of SAM the Summarizer. You decide what the better answer is, A or B.

1. Preparing to summarize: What is your assignment?

    A. Why did Mohandas Gandhi accept Thoreau's ideas and object to the governments in South Africa and India?

    B. Mohandas Gandhi disagreed with the term "passive resistance" to describe his actions in South Africa and India. Why do you think he would challenge the use of the phrase "passive resistance?"

    A is the only answer possible. Nowhere does the assignment use the question in answer choice B.

2. Analyze and decide what is important. There are six paragraphs. Put two paragraphs together and come up with important words, explanations, or opinions of the author that help to answer your assignment question.

    Paragraphs 1 and 2

    A. United States, Mexico, slavery, nonviolent options, lawbreakers, Jewel of the Crown, colonial power

    B. Thoreau, Civil Disobedience, nonviolent option, force the government, Gandhi, India, Great Britain, and suffering

B is the better answer because the selection is about how Thoreau's writings on civil disobedience helped to inspire Gandhi to stand up to the oppressive government of Great Britain.

Paragraphs 3 and 4

A. Hindu beliefs, emulate, law practice, legal advisor, racism and discrimination

B. Gandhi embraced British, lawyer, South Africa, racism and discrimination, injustice, and inhumanity

Again, B is the better answer. Think about how the words should tell the story happening in that paragraph. You can see that the words selected by the student in answer choice B show Gandhi moving from favoring the British to seeing racism in South Africa. The words in answer choice A are hard to even understand on their own and make it read as though he was Hindu and then practiced law. Don't pick words you don't understand. Find words that alone can be pieced together to recreate what the paragraph is saying.

Paragraphs 5 and 6

A. nonviolent resistance, winning battles, British landlords, non-cooperation, breaking salt laws, marchers, independence, Gandhi arrested, civil disobedience

B. superior military force, local struggle, Home Rule, Indian National Congress, monopoly, beach, breaking the law, talks

The better answer is A. The key words selected highlight Gandhi's resistance, winning of battles, breaking laws, marching and working toward independence. Answer choice B highlights fragmented words that read like vocabulary words but have no connection. What is Home Rule? What is the Indian National Congress and what does that have to do with a beach?

3. Map it out! Using the author's words, explanations, and opinions and your own words, summarize the answer to the assignment question.

A. Mohandas Gandhi used David Thoreau's idea of Civil Disobedience in his own life. He used nonviolence as a way to stand up against the British government ruling in India. At first, Gandhi liked the British government and followed all their rules. But when he left to practice law in South Africa and saw the racism and discrimination that the British were using there, he changed how he felt. He used nonviolence as a way to help the people of South Africa and then came back to India to do the same thing. He fought against British landlords and the monopoly the British had on salt production. He led marchers to the beach where they protested the salt laws. Even though Gandhi was arrested, he made it possible for others to protest using nonviolence.

B. Henry David Thoreau wrote a pamphlet about the United States and war in Mexico. He was against slavery and wanted nonviolent options to protest the government. Gandhi wanted the same thing in India against Great Britain. Gandhi was Hindu and a lawyer and didn't like the racism and discrimination he saw in South Africa. Gandhi came back to India. The British had a superior military force and Gandhi was in local struggles against the Indian National Congress. He fought against the monopoly and broke the laws and was able then to talk to the government.

A is the better answer. The student who wrote the summary in A used all the key words to recreate the story of Gandhi. The summary in B has information that isn't even correct because even though the words the student chose are from the reading selection, they don't go together correctly and don't explain what the selection is about.

Read the following selection about young adult author Chris Crutcher. Try all three reading organizers that we learned about in this chapter: Make an Inference, Text to Self Connections, and SAM the Summarizer.

Your Assignment: Answer the question: How did Chris Crutcher become a writer, and why does he write for young adults?

English Selection: "Connecting with Young Adult Writer Chris Crutcher" by Tony Sturgeon

Introduction

"What I'm going to do, as a writer, is make the best connection I can make with my characters. If I do that well, the kid will take it from there . . . I trust my readers to do that for themselves." As with many authors of young adult literature, Chris Crutcher feels the connection his stories have with his readers is the reason he is so popular with teenagers. However, Crutcher's connections are unique because he attempts to connect himself with his characters, which he feels will lead to a connection with the readers. This approach is one that has helped Chris Crutcher to become one of the most successful, and controversial, young adult authors writing today. The real question is, how is he able to make these connections with his characters? What has Chris Crutcher experienced that has contributed to this talent?

Chris Crutcher's Beginnings

After reading his novels that focus on issues such as racism, alcoholism, and school violence, one may think that Crutcher's upbringing was a turbulent one, especially since he claims to make connections with his characters. However, apart from having a mother who was an alcoholic, his family was the same as most of middle America's. Even his mother's alcoholism was tame when compared to the abusive drinkers that have appeared in his novels.

He is quick to point out that his mother's drinking did not keep her from holding a job and the "scars were not that deep."

Other aspects of Crutcher's teenage years were not that strange either. He grew up in a small town near Boise, Idaho, and because there was not much to do around the town, Chris found himself involved in sports, just like a lot of high school boys. He even continued this involvement as a member of the Eastern Washington State College swim team. Any reader of Crutcher's novels will be able to attest to the fact that he knows what it is like to be a competition swimmer, as many of his characters are also on their high school's swim teams. But simply being a member of a sports team will not make a person a successful novelist, although a strong academic career could be a step in the right direction.

Chris Crutcher and School

However, the academic facet of Chris Crutcher's life is less telling than the others. As a matter of fact, his performance in high school is exactly opposite of what you would have thought a successful novelist would have accomplished. When it came to reading, Crutcher avoided it like the plague. He only read one book his entire high school career, *To Kill a Mockingbird*. He claims he only read that book because at the time it was new and on the best-seller list. When it came to book reports, he often found himself making up titles and story lines, getting author's names from the telephone book, or copying the reports of his older brother, the valedictorian of his class. These are hardly the attributes of a future best-selling novelist. So once again, what led Chris Crutcher to write novels with such powerful characters?

Chris Crutcher's Careers

The real insight into Crutcher's connections with his teenage characters comes, surprisingly, more from his adult life and experiences than his own teenage years. Upon graduating from college with a teaching degree, Chris spent ten years as director of an alternative school in Oakland, California. During this time he spent much of his day dealing with troubled, inner-city children of all ages. There is little doubt that many of the things he saw and heard while serving as the school's director had an impact on the stories he would later write.

After spending a decade in California, Chris Crutcher moved back to Washington and found a job as a child and family therapist. He currently works in a mental health center where he focuses on child-abuse cases. He has dealt with children that have had to endure some of the worst experiences imaginable. Once again, his relationships and interactions with these families have allowed him to write more realistic stories to which young adults are drawn.

Chris Crutcher's Transition to Writing

Chris Crutcher did not begin writing until he was thirty-five years old. Since that time he has published nine young adult novels, one adult novel, numerous short-stories (including a collection of his own), and, most recently, an autobiography. When looking back at his own life, Crutcher agrees that what he has witnessed as a result of his career has allowed him to be a better author, or at least one that writes with realism. However, he does state that there is one important part of his teenage years, besides his involvement in sports, which has contributed to his writing. Chris says that he writes books that he would have liked to have read as a student. Crutcher claims that he was given the wrong stories to read, and that is why he never finished more than one book in high school. He hopes that his stories are ones that today's students will enjoy and share.

Final Thoughts on Chris Crutcher

As you can see, Chris Crutcher has not had one moment in his life that is dramatically different from most of us. He was a typical teenager, one that was not extremely successful in school. His adult life gave him the opportunity to see inside a world that is troublesome for many, but very real. His characters have come to reflect that reality. So how does Chris Crutcher make these connections with his characters? He answers that very simply, "The bottom line for me is to tell the truth . . . there's the connection."

MAKE AN INFERENCE

Choose a question from your reading
that hasn't been answered—something
you didn't understand. Then, using
clues in the text, add any background
knowledge (what you already know
about the topic) and answer the question. Make an inference.

1. What is an unanswered question
   you have from reading the story
   of Chris Crutcher? What do you
   know about Crutcher or any topic
   he discusses in the essay?
2. What kind of actual evidence
   (words, phrases, or sentences) can you find in the essay that
   might help you answer your question?
3. If you combine all the clues in the text with your background
   knowledge, can you answer your question?

TEXT TO SELF CONNECTIONS

Select a paragraph or passage from the Crutcher essay, and then
write down any connections you made between the text quota-
tions and your own life. Be as specific as possible.

1. Draw a picture of what you see in your head when you read
   the words in your chosen paragraph or passage.
2. What do you think those words mean?
3. How does it make you feel when you see those words?
4. Why do you think these words are important to understanding the meaning of the essay?

SAM THE SUMMARIZER

1. Preparing to summarize: What is your task? Rewrite it using
   your own words.
2. Analyze and decide what is important. There are six paragraphs. Put two paragraphs together and come up with
   important words, explanations, or opinions of the author
   that help to answer your assignment question.

3.   Map it out! Using the author's words, explanations, and opinions and your own words, summarize the answer to the assignment question, "How did Chris Crutcher become a writer, and why does he write for young adults?

HOW TEENS READ

Did you know that you forget up to fifty percent of what you read fifteen minutes after you read it? While you are reading, stop often to check that you understand what you are reading.

Several strategies can help you remember what you read:

- If you are getting bored with what you are reading but need to finish the reading assignment because you are running out of time, then read it aloud in different accents, like French or British. It's more fun that way, too!
- Imagine yourself as the character or as the person you are reading about.
- Stop and reread a passage if you don't get it.
- Start reading your assignment early so if you get tired, you can stop and come back to it later.
- Stop periodically and try summarizing in two sentences what you have just read. Say it out loud. Write it down or even text it to yourself!
- Carry your reading assignment around with you. When you have a few free minutes, read or reread a few pages. The more you read it, the more you will understand it.
- If you don't understand a word and you can't just skip it, then look it up in the glossary in the back of the book or on an online dictionary on your smartphone. Looking it up online is sometimes better because there are often pictures, and that helps you visualize what you are reading.
- Take breaks when you can't concentrate on your reading and there are millions of distracting voices in your head, or when you can't picture what you are reading.

Your reading attitude

It is important for your brain to be warmed before you read, but it's equally important that it remain warm while you read. If you don't keep your reading brain awake and alert, then the meaning of the words won't stick.

When you read, the text is talking to you. When a friend, your mom, or your teacher talks to you, you talk back. The same is true when you read. When the book is talking to you, talk back. Have a conversation. The Make an Inference, Text to Self Connections, and SAM the Summarizer are just notes from your conversation with the reading. They help to pull out the thoughts you would say back to the book if it were standing right in front of you saying what you are reading.

Mark Twain, a famous author, once said, "You cannot depend on your eyes when your imagination is out of focus." If you cannot imagine, then your eyes can't see. If your video camera is turned off and you aren't visualizing what you are reading, then you can't make sense of the words. Reading organizers help you see, feel, and think about the words you are reading so you can keep what you read in your head!

REFLECT ON WHAT YOU HAVE LEARNED!

1. Which one of the reading organizers—Make an Inference, Text to Self Connections, or SAM the Summarizer—worked best for you?
2. Why do you think it worked so well for you?
3. Which one or ones, then, will you add to your toolbox and use again?
4. Do you have a teen reading tip?
5. What *does* work for you when you are reading?
6. What *doesn't* work for you when you are reading?

BRAIN TICKLERS
Set # 3

Answer the following questions.
Remember to use the strategies discussed
in Chapter Two.

1. There are three types of voices that speak
   to you while you are reading. They are
   a. The word calling voice, the
      conversation voice, and the party
      voice.
   b. The conversation voice, the distracting
      voice, and the summarizer voice.
   c. The reciting voice, the party voice, and the word calling
      voice.
   d. The reciting voice, the conversation voice, and the
      distracting voice.

2. Making an inference is like
   a. Being a mathematician who is solving a math problem.
   b. Being a detective who looks for clues to solve a mystery.
   c. Being a writer who writes down his or her thoughts.
   d. Being a reader who reads for answers.

3. Good readers use many tools while reading, including which
   of the following:
   a. A video camera to record their thoughts and images
      while they read
   b. A paintbrush to paint their images
   c. A pencil or pen to write down their thoughts
   d. A book to read

(Answers are on page 54.)

BRAIN TICKLERS—THE ANSWERS

Set # 3, page 53

1. **d.** Remember, first you recite or say the words, then your conversation voice begins talking to the text. Your distracting voice, which may be thinking of a party, may interrupt your conversation voice.

2. **b.** When you make an inference, you read between the lines. You figure out what the author says based upon what clues he or she leaves in the text, so making an inference is most similar to being a detective.

3. **a.** Good readers are visualizing the images the words create and recording and remembering the words, which is what a video camera does. It helps make the people, events, and facts permanent.

CHAPTER FOUR

Decoding Versus Reading

DO YOU REALLY GET WHAT YOU ARE READING?

Read this selection out loud.

> Guten Tag. Wie geht es ihnen? Ich bin gut. Meine name is Frau Jones. Ich bin der Autor vom *Painless Reading Comprehension*. Ich lese sehr gern. Dieses buch liest sich gut.

Would you say that you can read the passage? Probably you can say the words, but is that reading? The only "words" you really know and understand are *Painless Reading Comprehension* because they are English. Reading is more than just saying the words. You have to understand what you read while you read. So, unless you know German as I do, you probably have no idea what the passage means.

Here is the translation:

> Hello, how are you? My name is Mrs. Jones. I am the author of *Painless Reading Comprehension*. I am fond of reading. This book is a good book to read.

Understanding what you read

Because reading is more than just saying the words, you have to understand what you read while you read. In Chapter Three, we looked at the different types of voices that speak to you while you read. As you recall, the reciting voice is the voice you hear when you are only "word calling" or just decoding the words. You don't understand what you are reading. And you might be able to decode entire passages or pages fluently but not comprehend or remember what you read. Don't confuse decoding with reading. They aren't the same thing.

When you first learned to read, your teachers praised you when you could pronounce the words. Back then, you were learning how letters formed words and sounds, so saying the words *was* a big deal and *was* considered reading. But, as you grow and learn more, reading means something different. Now you need to be able to put all the words in a passage together and solve the message. That is what reading really is—understanding the message the author is sending to you, the reader.

Literacy is reading and writing. Being literate means you can read and write. If you are illiterate, you cannot read or write. As time has evolved so has the idea of what is literate. When the United States was first forming, someone was considered literate if he or she could sign their name. After that, people were considered literate if they could copy documents and spell and read simple words. Before World War II, people were considered literate if they could memorize popular and classic literature—decode. After World War II and even up to just twenty years ago, comprehension or knowing the message and understanding the plot and characters became more important than memorization.

Critical literacy. But you are now living in what is called the critical literacy era, in which, you, the student, are being asked not only to sign, copy, read, spell, write, and comprehend but also to analyze, interpret, and criticize what you are reading and writing. In fact, the Common Core and state standards and curricula of almost all schools reflect this new literacy, so you are expected to be able read and write critically in every subject. You are lucky because this type of literacy is hands-on and allows for all perspectives to be recognized as important; however, it also asks you to be a more responsive reader, which means that you have to give and show more reading effort.

HOW DO YOU CONNECT WITH THE WORDS?

Reading is like a jigsaw puzzle. Now, some of you are probably saying, "No kidding, it's a puzzle I can't always find the pieces to!" To put a puzzle together, you first need to find the edge pieces and lay them down. They are the easiest to find because of their shape. Then, you need to work your way inward, studying the colors and shapes on the individual pieces and fitting together colors and shapes with similar colors and shapes. When you read, you first need to read the text in parts and then read it as a whole. In other words, you must break it down and then put the pieces together. In the remainder of this chapter, you will learn strategies for how to do just that!

FLAG WORDS

When you receive an important or urgent email or text, you may notice a flag attached to it. Or when you are shopping online picking out things you want for your birthday, you may bookmark it as important. Likewise, when you read, certain words signal you, alert you, or clue you in about how what you are reading is structured. Let's look at the jigsaw puzzle analogy.

Flag words are similar to the pieces that outline the frame or skeleton of the puzzle and allow you to see more easily how the puzzle will be put together. For example, *Until you clean your room, you can't go to the mall.* The word *until* tells you that there will be something else that you will be reading. The word *until* is a flag that you are about to read a sequence of events. *Until you clean your room* is one event and *you can't go to the mall* is a second event.

Flag words can be broken down into many categories. Here are five of the most frequently used categories:

- cause and effect
- comparison and contrast
- emphasis
- illustration
- sequence

Cause and effect

Cause is an action, and the effect is that action's outcome. An example flag word for cause and effect is *because*. *Because you are reading this book, you will become a better reader.* The effect, becoming a better reader, is a result of the cause, reading this book.

Some other common cause-and-effect flag words are

therefore	since
so that	as a result of
consequently	if . . . then

Comparison and contrast

When you compare something, you tell what is similar about two or more ideas. When you contrast something, you tell what is different about two or more ideas. One flag word for comparison and contrast is *likewise*. For example, *Reading often is the best way to better your vocabulary skills. Likewise, writing is a vocabulary builder.* When you see the word *likewise*, you know the writer is going to compare vocabulary skill building to something else besides reading, which in this case happens to be writing. A contrast word is *but*. For example, *Teaching vocabulary with word lists is a good method, but using word lists while reading a story with the words is even better.* The word *but* contrasts the two ideas: teaching vocabulary with just word lists and teaching vocabulary with word lists for a story.

Some other common comparison and contrast flag words are:

like	differ or difference
equally	on the contrary
in the same way	on the other hand
similarly	otherwise
for example	regardless
just as	whereas
however	than

Emphasis words

Emphasis words are words that let you know that what the writer is saying is especially important and he or she wants you to pay close attention. When you are in class and taking notes, your teacher may tell you exactly what he or she wants you to write down or may repeat something and give you time to write that statement down. Writers do the same thing, but you must be able to recognize the flag word the author uses so you know what is really noteworthy. For example, *The many events of World War II, such as the battle on Normandy, the French invasion, and the war front in Africa are significant, but the most important event for Americans is the bombing of Pearl Harbor because it catapulted the Americans into the war.* The flag words *most important event* tell the reader that the next event is the idea the writer wants you, the reader, to really focus on and think about.

Some other common emphasis words are:

> a significant feature, event, or factor
>
> remember that
>
> above all
>
> important to note
>
> especially important or valuable
>
> should be noted
>
> a key feature, factor, or event
>
> a distinctive quality or feature
>
> a primary concern

Illustration words

Now the word *illustration* doesn't mean you are going to see actual pictures on the page, but you will develop pictures in your head. Illustration words tell you that the writer is going to illustrate or give you examples or ideas of what he or she means. Illustration words give you a clue that an example that you can picture in your head is about to be read. For example, *We take pictures all the time, but we don't always have a camera. For example, think of your first day at school. You can remember that day even if you don't have an actual photograph.* The flag words, *for example,* illustrate what the writer means when she says, *We take pictures all the time, but we don't always have a camera.* If we just stopped reading there and didn't bother to read her illustration, we might be confused. As you have probably noticed, I use *for example* all the time. You know by now that when I say those two words, I am going to explain what my last statement means.

Some other common illustration words are:

> for instance
>
> to illustrate
>
> such as

Sequence words

Sequence words are flag words that writers use to explain several related items in a series. Sequence words let you know what the first item is, the items in between are, and the final item is in the list. For example, *First you need to grease a 9 × 13 inch pan. Then, you need to place flour in the pan and move the flour around so that it sticks to the butter. Finally, dump the excess flour out.* The words *first, then,* and *finally* tell you what you need to do or what will happen first, second, and so on. Sequence words are used often to describe an event or to explain a process.

Some other common sequence words are:

first	lastly
second	then
third	next
finally	in addition

Read the following sentence:

Cracks in the highway concrete surface are a result of ice freezing and melting and breaking down the concrete's composition.

The questions below will ask you to do one of three tasks: identify the flag word in the sentence, explain what category the flag word fits under, or detail what important information the flag word is highlighting for you.

1. What is the flag word?
   a. a result of
   b. breaking down
   c. freezing and melting
   d. melting and breaking

The answer is a. *If you look at the list of flag words on page 60, you will clearly see this phrase listed.*

2. What category is the flag word?
   a. Comparison and Contrast
   b. Emphasis
   c. Cause and Effect
   d. Illustration

The answer is c. *The words "a result of" indicate that something came first and the result or effect is something else.*

3. What important information is the flag word highlighting?
   a. Ice freezes and melts
   b. Cracks in the highway are caused by ice freezing and melting
   c. Ice breaks down concrete
   d. Roads are made out of concrete

The answer is b. *When you reread the sentence, you know that the problem or consequence—the cracks in the highway—are caused by ice freezing and melting. Answer choices a and c are true but not complete answers. Answer choice d has nothing to do with the question.*

BRAIN TICKLERS
Set # 4

Now you try! Read the paragraph and answer the questions below. Remember to use the strategies discussed earlier in the book and remember the answers can be found at the end of the chapter.

(1) It should be noted that along with food production, human beings found time to develop the arts and sciences. (2) Some hunter-gatherers must have had considerable leisure without making any notable movement toward civilization. (3) A difference between the hunter-gatherers and farmers that is important to note is that the former are usually nomadic whereas the latter are sedentary. (4) But even those pre-agricultural people who had fairly stationary living sites did not develop in civilizing ways comparable to the farmers.

1. What is the flag word in sentence number 1?
   a. along with
   b. noted
   c. should be noted
   d. to develop

2. In what category does the flag word "difference" in sentence number 3 belong?
   a. Emphasis
   b. Comparison and Contrast
   c. Illustration
   d. Sequence Words

3. What important information is the author detailing with the flag word "but" in sentence number 4?

  a. Even though pre-agricultural people had fairly stationary living sites, they still did not develop in civilizing ways comparable to the farmers.

  b. The farmers were more civilized.

  c. Pre-agricultural people had stationary living sites.

  d. Pre-agricultural people lived before farmers.

(Answers are on page 83.)

HELP WITH VOCABULARY

Parlez Vous Francais?

The word *vocabulary* refers to the words used in a language and the sum of those words used by a particular person or group within that language. Therefore, understanding those words and the sum of those words is very important to understanding what you are reading. If you don't know what the words mean, then it's hard to solve the puzzle. When you are reading, you may feel like you are reading a foreign language because the words look so strange to you.

Let's look at how we learn what words mean. Before you went to school, you learned new words by listening to the adults and other kids around you talk. You tried out new words, associated meaning with them, and then learned to put the words into meaningful sentences to form a message. At school, your teachers helped you to build your vocabulary by giving you lists of words, asking you to define them, spell them, and maybe do activities like use the words in sentences. Your teachers also read to you and asked you to read on your own. All of those events, listening, speaking, memorizing, and reading, have helped your vocabulary to grow. There are millions of words out there, and no one expects you to know them all—you just need to know how to figure out what they mean!

Think of a word as a jigsaw puzzle piece. By itself, it has its own color and shape. Just like a word on its own, it has meaning. Think of the word *heart.* On its own, you might think of the organ beating in your chest, pushing blood through your body. However, once I connect that word to other words, it may take on a different meaning. The same is true with a puzzle. When you snap a puzzle piece into the puzzle, it takes on a different meaning as well and becomes something different than what it started out being. For example,

> *The firefighters at the scene of the Twin Towers in New York City on 9/11 showed great heart in saving so many lives.*

When you snap the word "heart" into place along with other words, it takes on a new meaning. The word "heart" in the sentence isn't talking about an organ; it's talking about courage and bravery.

Connotation and denotation

Words have two identities: connotation and denotation. When you read a word on its own, you think of the dictionary definition—*denotation*. But, when you read a word in context (connected to other words), it may take on a new meaning—*connotation*. When I say the word "heart," we may all agree on a standard definition or its denotation, which is an organ in the body. However, when you reread the sentence

> *The firefighters at the scene of the Twin Towers in New York City on 9/11 showed great heart in saving so many lives.*

we think of a new definition. In fact, when we read words, we naturally think and visualize other meanings based upon our personal experiences. For example, upon hearing the word "heart," someone might see her grandfather lying in a hospital bed after he had heart surgery. Someone else might see a person he loves. Someone else might see her favorite basketball hero who showed great spirit or heart when he helped his team win the game. In fact, probably not too many of us visualize a body organ.

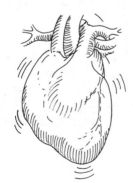

That's part of the problem with vocabulary. When you read something unfamiliar to you,

you either don't know what the words mean or you don't know what definitions of the words the writer wants you to use. Read the following passage.

Portraitures

Before you begin shooting professional portraitures, you must first take a meter reading. Find out how much light is around and on the subject or subjects you are shooting. Before you set the dials on your camera, decide how much depth of field you want. Do you only want the subject or subjects in the photo to be in focus or do you want what is surrounding the subject to also be in focus? If you only want the human subject or subjects to be in focus (short depth of field), then open your aperture or F stops up (1.4, 2.8, or 5.6) and set your shutter fast (60, 125, or 250). If you want everything to be in focus, then close your aperture down (8.0, 11.0, or 16.0) and set your shutter slow (30 or 15).

Now, you probably figured out that this passage is talking about taking pictures, but unless you are a photographer, you don't know much else. When you read something and don't understand it, you feel like an outsider to the topic—a foreigner in a foreign land! And, when you try to figure out what a word means by looking at it on its own, by figuring out its denotation only, you still don't know what it means. You must do more than that. You need to be an insider to the topic and figure out what the word means on its own and what it means while it is connected or hooked into other words. This may take some time, but it's well worth the effort.

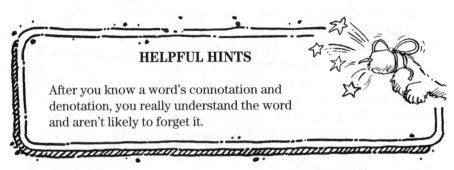

HELPFUL HINTS

After you know a word's connotation and denotation, you really understand the word and aren't likely to forget it.

Vocabulary strategies

Here are some strategies that can help you figure out the meaning of words. First of all, most writers will give you clues as to what a word means. Let's look at the jigsaw puzzle again. When you look at an individual puzzle piece, you may have some idea of what part of the overall image that piece represents, but you will not know for certain until you look at the pieces around that piece.

When you see an individual word, you are faced with four possible scenarios:

- You have never seen or heard the word before.
- You have seen or heard the word before but aren't sure what it means.
- You have seen or heard the word before and know what it means.
- You have seen or heard the word before and know several meanings of the word.

The last scenario isn't a problem that needs solving. The fact is, you know many definitions of most of the words you read. Think about it. When you are reading, you know the majority of the words; usually only a handful of words trip you up. But those few words can be enough to scramble the message the writer is trying to send you. The following problem-solving strategies will help you with the first three scenarios that occur while you are reading.

READING CONTEXT CLUES AND SOLVING THE PUZZLE

When you are reading and get stuck on a word, skip it. Ask yourself whether the rest of the sentence makes sense without it. Can you understand the sentence without knowing what that word means? When you read, don't expect to know what every single word means. No one expects you to be a human dictionary! But, if you don't understand the writer's message and you need to understand what the word means, then try this. See if you can figure out what the word means in context. You may have heard your teachers tell you to use the context or the context clues. Context clues are the words around the word you are trying to decipher.

I immediately recognized the inaccurate information because the writer used research that was spurious.

Sometimes the writer will tell you what the word means by restating the meaning directly after the word. For example,

> She is a vivacious girl, full of life.

Vivacious means full of life.

Sometimes the writer will give you the definition in the next sentence. For example,

> When creating a scrapbook, be sure to use archival paper. Archival paper will last forever because it is acid free and won't fade or crumble.

In the first sentence, you stumbled over the word *archival*. But after you read the next sentence, you understood that archival paper is paper that can be preserved.

Writers also help you to understand a difficult word by giving you the opposite meaning. For example,

> Mary was defiant, but her twin sister was cooperative.

You may not know what the word *defiant* means, but you understand *cooperative*. And, you know by the way the sentence is set up with the use of the word *but* that Mary is different from her twin. So, because you know that one sister is cooperative or helpful and easy to get along with, you infer that Mary is defiant or difficult to get along with.

Here is another example.

> So far, the evidence presented at the trial has been insignificant, but her testimony proved to be poignant and marked a turning point in the trial.

You may not know what *poignant* means, but you know that *insignificant* means not important so *poignant* must mean important. The writer says that the testimony *marked a turning point in the trial,* which means something important happened at the trial so the *poignant* testimony must have been important.

Let's Practice!

Read the following sentences. Using the context clues strategies to define the words flepid, abert, *and* vemoxly. *Also, describe the strategies you used to figure out those words.*

John was always flepid and excited when it came time to discuss politics.

Susan's use of abert marked a change in the way scientists viewed laboratory testing. Abert, a part vinegar and part salt solution, was a remarkable way to see faster results.

Because of his disorganized locker, uncombed hair, and generally sloppy appearance, everyone was shocked when Ryan came to school dressed so vemoxly.

Guess what? Those words are nonsensical! There are no such words as *flepid, abert,* and *vemoxly.* But, I wanted you to see that even if a word looks really strange to you and you have never heard or seen it before, you can still figure out what it means.

Let's Practice!

Read the following passage about artist Faith Ringgold. There are three sentences in italics. Within each of those three sentences, there is a word that is underlined. When you see those three sentences and the three words, use the context clues discussed earlier in this chapter to assign meaning to the difficult word so that you can understand the sentence in the text.

Art and English Selection: "The Powerful Work and Words of Faith Ringgold" by Julie Strawhacker

Faith Ringgold's art and words, both written and spoken, have a powerful effect upon any person who is fortunate enough to experience them, myself included. In 1993, after hearing Maya Angelou read her poem at President Clinton's inauguration and seeing Ringgold's art quilt called *Tar Beach*, I was inspired to create a quilt of my own using Angelou's words. The quilt contains the poem within its border and faces of people from different racial backgrounds painted as petals of intertwining flowers in the fabric pattern in its center. I was presented with the opportunity to meet Faith Ringgold for the first time on April 3, 1995, as she was introduced to me, first by the flyer I had received in my painting class at Ball State University, announcing her visit, and then later by name as she shared her time discussing my work with me. *I immediately felt Faith Ringgold's presence; the presence of a proud and confident woman, like no other I had known before. It filled the room and me with a powerful energy.* [Sentence 1]

I waited for my turn, took a deep breath, and shared with Ringgold how her unique way of creating the *Tar Beach* had inspired my work. She, in return, expressed her approval of my quilt and the admiration she had for the work of Maya Angelou and thanked me for sharing my quilt with her. The apprehension I felt before she spoke was immediately erased and replaced with admiration and gratitude. *I will always remember her gentle demeanor as she listened, speaking with a quiet kindness that was meant only for me.* [Sentence 2] *I greatly admire Faith Ringgold for her sincere kindness to me as a young artist, and also for her conviction as a black female artist who has the courage to speak with honesty and great wisdom.* [Sentence 3] Never have I heard someone speak so candidly to a group of art students and teachers, including myself. The slides of her work, along with her words, provoked questions within me while providing some answers that had been missing from my limited education of United States History, specifically the gaps involving the struggles of African American people. I have been educated and emotionally changed because of Faith Ringgold.

Ringgold has found much success as an artist, including receiving more than seventy-five awards and seventeen honorary doctorates of fine arts, both National Endowment of the Arts and the Guggenheim fellowships and having her work in the collections of the New York City Metropolitan Museum of Art, the Museum of Modern Art, and the Studio Museum in Harlem. Today, her work appears in a variety of public places as a result of various commissions, some of which include murals that reside in the 125th Street Harlem subway station, a Brooklyn school library, a Women's House of Detention on Riker's Island, and Bronx College and a quilt in the Crown Heights Public Library.

1. What is the difficult word in sentence 1?
   - What does that word mean?
   - What context clues strategy did you use to assign the word meaning?

2. What is the difficult word in sentence 2?
   - What does that word mean?
   - What context clues strategy did you use to assign the word meaning?

3. What is the difficult word in sentence 3?
   - What does that word mean?
   - What context clues strategy did you use to assign the word meaning?

Let's Practice!

Now, it's your turn to be the writer. Create three new words. Have some fun and make them really strange. Place each made-up word into three different sentences. Use the context clues strategies outlined earlier.

1. Give the definition within the sentence.
2. Give the definition in the next sentence.
3. Give the opposite definition within the sentence.
4. See if your friends can "read" your words and tell you what they mean.

HELPFUL HINTS

What if there are no flag words to help explain the passage? What if you can't figure out what a word means by using the context? What if you don't know what the word's connotation or denotation is? One tried-and-true solution is to look it up!

Deciphering the dictionary

How many times have you asked
your teacher what a word means
and the teacher said, "Look it
up!" So, after you finally find the
dictionary, you aren't sure how
to find the word and so you ask
someone else in the class for
help. Has this happened to you?
Using a dictionary can be confusing, but it is an important and
necessary skill that you will use
forever. Even if you look online
and not in an actual book, you

still must understand what you are looking at. If you don't know
how to use a dictionary, finding the word can be difficult, and
then when you do find the word, the entry can look like it was
written in a foreign language.

Inside the dictionary

Grab a dictionary or use an online dictionary, and follow along
with me. Words in a text dictionary are arranged alphabetically.
In the top left corner of each page of a dictionary, you will see
the first word on that dictionary page. In the top right corner of
each dictionary page, you will see the last word on that dictionary
page. If you use this structure, you can see the alphabetical range
of words on those two pages and can more quickly find the word
you are looking for. The larger dictionaries with many words
have alphabet tabs on the side so that you can more easily access
the first letter of the word. For online dictionaries, you simply
have to type in the word you want defined and it will appear.
However, both online and text dictionaries use the same format
for entering words.

Look at the following entry from *www.dictionary.com* for
the word *decipher*, which appears in the following sentence:
Sheila *deciphered* the math problem by using the same method
as the teacher had shown them in class.

de•ci•pher (dĭ-sī'fᵊr)
tr.v. **de•ci•phered, de•ci•pher•ing, de•ci•phers**

1. To read or interpret (ambiguous, obscure, or illegible matter).
2. To convert from a code or cipher to plain text; decode.

de•ci'pher•a•ble *adj.*
de•ci'pher•er *n.*
de•ci'pher•ment *n.*

Let me help you decipher the dictionary entry for *decipher*. After the word *decipher*, in parentheses, is the pronunciation guide: (dĭ-sī'fᵊr). The *tr.v* means it is a transitive verb. Transitive verbs have a direct object; in other words, you can answer who or what after the verb. After the *tr.v* are common but different versions of the word *decipher*. And the numbers 1. and 2. precede the definitions of the word. Below the 1. and 2. are again other versions of the word that are commonly used. For your purpose of looking up the meanings or denotations of words, we will concern ourselves with the part of speech, the commonly used versions of the word, and the definitions.[8]

Parts of speech

There are eight parts of speech. Most of the words you look up will be nouns, verbs, adjectives, or adverbs. Remember, nouns are persons, places, things, or ideas; verbs are words that take action either in your head or with your body; adjectives give extra information about or describe nouns; and adverbs give extra information about or describe verbs. You need to know the part of speech so that you can identify if the word is the subject or object, if the word is tying the subject to an action, or if the word is describing. For example, since you know that *decipher* is a verb, you can look to see what is being deciphered, which helps you to understand that *decipher* is an action. When you look up the word, first see what part of speech it is and then reread the word in the sentence.

Versions of the word

The word you are looking up may not appear in the dictionary exactly as it does on your page. Make sure you are looking up the correct word by reviewing the different versions of the word.

Definitions

Finally, read the definitions. Often the first definition is the best definition because it is the most commonly used definition. But, sometimes you will read a definition that simply repeats the word you are looking up, which doesn't help! So you must read on until you read a definition that makes sense to you.

HELPFUL HINTS

Tips on using the dictionary
- Use the same text or online dictionary consistently to become familiar with the format in that dictionary.
- If you are using a textbook, look up the word in the glossary first because it will provide the exact meaning the author intended for what you are reading.

STAIRCASE TO VOCABULARY SUCCESS

When you walk up a set of stairs, you move closer to your goal of reaching the top. Think about learning new words in terms of a set of steps. The bottom step is the word. Your goal is to figure out what the word means. The meaning is at the top step. If you are reading a passage and come across a word that you don't know the meaning of, then try climbing the staircase to success. At the first step, look the word up in the dictionary. Remember to use the first or second definitions first because they are the most common meanings.

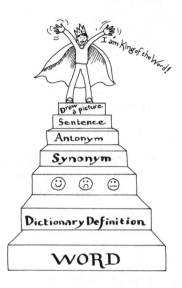

At the second step, decide if the definition has a positive connotation, a neutral connotation, or a negative connotation. Recall our discussion of all the different connotations associated with the word *heart*? The word *heart* has a positive connotation because, as we noted earlier, we think of it as one of the most important organs in our body, relate it to having great spirit, or associate it with love. Connotation is the definition and meaning *you* associate with the word. A word that has a negative connotation would be the word *plague*. Even though you may not know the exact definition for *plague*, you know it is a bad thing. You know it has a negative connotation. A *plague* is a widespread disease or sickness. The word *software* has a neutral connotation. *Software* is the program you place on your computer. We don't really have a positive or negative feeling toward software; therefore, it's neutral. When you see those three words, you can mentally assign them faces that express their connotation.

At the third step, provide a synonym for the word. A synonym is a word that has the same meaning or nearly the same meaning as the word you are defining. For example, a synonym for *confidant*, who is someone you can tell your secrets to, is *friend*.

At the fourth step, offer an antonym for the word. An antonym is a word that has the opposite meaning of the word you are defining. For example, an antonym for the word *confidant* would be *enemy*. The words synonym and antonym can be confusing. Just remember *synonym* means *same* and antonym means opposite.

At the fifth step, use the word in a sentence. For example,

> *Because Fonda was my closest confidant, I told her my secret.*

When you read a word you don't understand and you look it up and use the word, you are committing it to memory. By taking all these steps, you are ensuring that you probably won't have to ever look this word up again!

The final step, the last step before the top of the staircase, is fun. Draw a picture of the word! This isn't art class, and no one expects you to be van Gogh. All you have to do is roughly sketch out the image that appears in your head.

This may seem like too much work to learn one word. But, not understanding just one word can confuse the writer's entire message. Climbing the staircase guarantees you reach your goal of learning the word. Not only will you learn the single word, but you will better understand what you read, which means you will do well on your work for school. The staircase is a good exercise to use when studying for vocabulary tests for any subject and foreign language tests as well.

Let's Practice!

Here is a passage about a famous short story. Read the passage and then climb the vocabulary steps for the three words that are underlined.

In the short story, "Metamorphosis" by Franz Kafka, the main character undergoes a metamorphosis from a man into a cockroach. Kafka's tale is surreal, yet it is a metaphor for how low man can go if he forgets he has as much power to be great as he does to be nothing.

Read some more about Ringgold's artistic choices. When you see a word underlined, create a vocabulary staircase for that word.

Ringgold's artistic themes dealing with racial and feminist issues and her desire to address social and political problems were not considered to be a part of the mainstream art of the 1960's and therefore were another roadblock to her gaining recognition as a legitimate artist. The mainstream art of the 1960's was a cool and detached product, not a vehicle for communicating ideas to viewers.

Many artists, both black and white, held this as an ideal way to create. The Social Realist style of Faith Ringgold's *American People Series* and other similar works was seen as being out of touch with the artistic trend of the time. Ringgold comments: "Issue oriented art was dismissed as being naïve, if not down right vulgar. Art was a conceptual or material process, a commodity and not a political platform."

Ringgold also dealt with stylistic problems when attempting to render faces of both black and white people similarly. She experimented with flat, stylized shapes with less attention to realism and perspective that drew influence from both African Masks and Cubist faces. She used this new style in painting both black and white people, avoiding the negative connotation of <u>caricature</u> drawings of people of African descent by rendering both in the same manner. These renderings of people consist of groupings of curves and interconnected oval shapes.

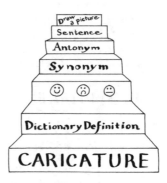

REFLECT ON WHAT YOU HAVE LEARNED!

1. Which vocabulary strategies worked best for you?
2. Which tools will you add to your toolbox?
3. Why do you think they are good tools for you?

BRAIN TICKLERS
Set # 5

Use the strategies you learned in Chapter Two to figure out the answers to the following multiple-choice questions.

1. Remember, flag words are words that signal you, alert you, or clue you in about the meaning of what you are reading. In the following sentence, what is the flag word and the category that the flag word falls into? *It is important to note that taking notes and summarizing are two of the most important strategies to use for academic success.*
   a. *Most* and emphasis
   b. *Important to note* and illustration
   c. *Important* and cause and effect
   d. *Important to note* and emphasis

2. You can define a word by both its denotation and connotation. What is the denotation of a word?
   a. The feeling of the word
   b. The meaning the reader gives the word
   c. The dictionary definition of a word
   d. The connotation of the word

3. What context clue would you use to figure out what the word *spurious* means in the following sentence? *I immediately recognized the spurious nature of the writing because the research the writer used was inaccurate information.*

   a. The writer restates the word's meaning in the same sentence.
   b. The writer explains what the word means in the next sentence.
   c. The writer provides an opposite meaning of the word.
   d. The writer uses the flag word *because* to explain the word.

(Answers are on page 83.)

BRAIN TICKLERS—THE ANSWERS

Set # 4, page 64

1. **c.** The phrase "should be noted" is used to call attention to an important point. It is used for emphasis.

2. **b.** When you discuss the difference between two things, you are contrasting them.

3. **a.** The flag word "but" contrasts one piece of information with another. "But" says that while one piece of information is true, another piece of information is equally true.

Set # 5, page 81

1. **d.** All the answers use correct words and categories, but only one matches to answer the twofold question. Something that is important to note would be something that is worth emphasizing.

2. **c.** Remember denotation goes with dictionary. To denote a word is to define it. Connotation is the meaning we associate with a word.

3. **a.** There is only one sentence and no negating words, only the word *because*, which leads you to an explanation of what the word means.

CHAPTER FIVE

Keeping What You Read in Your Head

WHAT DO I DO WHEN I AM
FINISHED READING?

What do you do when you are finished reading and you have to complete an assignment, prepare for a discussion, or study for a quiz or test, but you can't remember all that you have read? How do you keep what you have read in your head?

Have you ever read something and thought you understood the reading but realized you didn't know the answers to the assignment? Of course, this has happened to you. It has happened to everyone!

Remember when we talked about your reading brain being alert and awake, napping, or drooling while you read? You may think you are alert while you are reading, but sometimes your brain wanders and you don't realize it. You may be alert at the beginning and alert or awake periodically throughout the reading but napping—maybe even drooling—at other times. You only registered the alert and awake times. So, to recall what you read, you may need to

- Go back and skim for the information you need OR
- Go back, reread, and take notes.

Now that may sound like a lot of work, but it doesn't have to be. Here are some tips on how to skim and reread.

SKIMMING FOR INFORMATION

When you skim for information, you are just trying to quickly reconnect yourself with a section or a part of the reading. Readers skim when some time has passed between when they read the material and when they have to study or do an assignment. They may also skim if they were napping through a section instead of being alert when they read. For example, even though you read about Agnes Vogel's life as a Holocaust survivor and are familiar with her story, you may have to know the date she was liberated. So you go back and skim for the answer.

When you skim, you are looking for certain information in a specific section. Readers don't usually skim the entire selection!

Here are some strategies for skimming:

- If you are skimming for information in a novel, use the chapter titles as a guide.
- If you are skimming in a textbook, use the Table of Contents, boldfaced headings, or the section outline in the chapter. If the question refers to a particular section, then you only need to skim in that section.
- If you are skimming an article, use paragraph indentations as a guide to a new idea. The first two sentences are usually the topic sentences and will quickly tell you what the paragraph is about.
- If you are looking for numbers or dates, skim for numbers only.
- If you are skimming to find the meaning of a certain word or phrase, then skim for the word or phrase and then read the sentences immediately before and after the sentence the word or phrase is in to get the information you need. If you are reading something online or digitially, you can use the "Find" feature to find the word or phrase.

Sometimes you have to use two or more of these to get one answer.

Let's work through a discussion guide assignment for "Agnes Vogel: Survivor from Hungary" and the reading selection itself. You read about Mrs. Vogel's experiences in Chapter Two, but it has been a while. Go back to Chapter Two, find the reading selection, and skim to find the answers to the following specific questions.

AGNES VOGEL DISCUSSION QUESTIONS

1. Where is Agnes Vogel from? What was her life like prior to the war?
2. Which camp was Vogel in right before liberation? Compare her life in that camp with her life in the camp at Strasoff.
3. What year was Vogel liberated and by whom?
4. What did Vogel's family find when they returned to their home?
5. What does Vogel mean when she says the Nazis were "liquidating the Ghetto?"

REFLECT ON WHAT YOU HAVE LEARNED!

What skimming strategy did you use to answer question 1: *Where is Agnes Vogel from? What was her life like prior to the war?*

You should have looked under the boldfaced heading titled "Agnes' Early and Happy Life" to find your answer.

What skimming strategy did you use for question 2: *Which camp was Vogel in right before liberation? Compare her life in that camp with her life in the camp at Strasoff.*

You had to use two steps. First, you should have found the section titled "Liberation" and looked at the section of reading prior to that, which was titled "The Death Camp: Bergen Belsen." You know that was the camp she was in prior to liberation. Then, you had to find the section where you saw the word *Strasoff.* You probably guessed it might be in the section titled "The Concentration Camp." And by reading the first topic sentence, your guess can be validated. After skimming those two sections, you could answer the question.

What skimming strategy did you use for question 3: *What year was Vogel liberated and by whom?*

You had to look under the section titled "Liberation" and then look for a date. After you found a date, you had to read the sentence before, the sentence the date was in, and the sentence after the date to make sure the date was referring to liberation.

What skimming strategy did you use for question 4: *What did Vogel's family find when they returned to their home?*

To answer this question, you had to look for the section titled "Journey Home."

What skimming strategy did you use for question 5: *What does Vogel mean when she says the Nazis were "liquidating the Ghetto?"*

This is again a two-step process. First, you had to look under the section titled "War, Persecution, and the Ghetto." You infer that since this section has the word *Ghetto* in the title, it will probably have the information you need. Then, you skim for the phrase *liquidating the Ghetto*. Once you find that phrase, you read the sentence before the phrase, the sentence the phrase is in, and the sentence after the phrase to get the information you need.

Let's Practice!

Go back to page 47 and find the reading selection on Chris Crutcher. Skim the passage to find the answers to the following questions.

1. Chris Crutcher states that his gift as a writer is being able to connect to what part of his books?
   a. The plot
   b. The characters
   c. The message

2. What was Chris Crutcher's life like growing up?

3. What was the only book Chris Crutcher read in high school?

4. How old was Chris Crutcher when he started writing?

5. True or False: Chris Crutcher was a therapist before becoming a writer.

REFLECT ON WHAT YOU HAVE LEARNED!
What skimming strategy did you use to answer question 1?
What skimming strategy did you use to answer question 2?
What skimming strategy did you use to answer question 3?
What skimming strategy did you use to answer question 4?
What skimming strategy did you use to answer question 5?

REREADING PART OF THE TEXT

What if you have to know by memory the information in the reading assignment for a discussion, quiz, or test? What if there is no assignment and your teacher has told you to just study and know the information? How do you know what you are supposed to know? How do you know what is important? You might think that if you read it once, you know it. But, that's not possible.

HELPFUL HINTS

Even the very best readers must reread and take notes to remember what they read.

Unless you are the author or an expert in the topic, there is no way you can know everything you read.

When I was in high school, I received some very good advice from a teacher. I had performed poorly on a quiz about a novel we were reading in class and I asked the teacher what I had done wrong.

"But, I read the chapter and listened in class!" I insisted.

"Apparently you were not reading or listening closely enough," said Mrs. M.

And I retorted, "Well, no offense Mrs. M., but this stuff is boring!"

And Mrs. M., unmoved by my smart aleck and defensive remark, replied, "If you are bored while you read or listen, then take notes—it keeps your brain awake so you don't get bored!"

Taking notes

I thought about that, tried it, and it worked! Mrs. M. was right. (Teachers generally are!) Taking notes keeps your hands moving, which guarantees that your brain will stay awake and alert and keeps you connected to the words and their meaning,

When you sleep, your body temperature drops. The same is true with your reading brain. When you are reading or listening and your alert or awake brain changes to napping or drooling, your brain goes cold. When your brain goes cold, *rigor mortis* can set in and no meaning can penetrate.

Think about it! We have all stayed up really late reading a book or a magazine because we just couldn't stop reading. When we are really into something, our brain is not just warm—it's hot!

Not everything you read will be interesting to you. Not everything will make your brain hot or even warm, but you need to read to learn! So take notes!

Whenever I find myself getting bored or napping while I am reading or listening to a presentation, I stop, reread, and take notes. By doing something with my hands and my brain, I can stay focused and keep what I read in my head.

RADAR

So, how do you take notes? You turn on and use your reading RADAR: read, anticipate, decide, analyze, record. Radar focuses in on something specific. An air traffic controller uses radar to see exactly where planes are in the sky. Ground troops in the military use ground surveillance radar to detect enemy movement of troops or vehicles. Bats even use a type of radar. They can't see, but they emit sound waves that work like radar. When the

How do you take... they can't see... But... sends sound back... allowing them to see...

sound hits an object, it sends the sound back to the bat allowing the bat to "see" the object ahead.

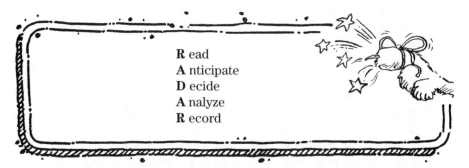

R ead
A nticipate
D ecide
A nalyze
R ecord

Using reading radar is an effective way to reread and find the important ideas. RADAR allows you to see all the words on the page and to focus in on only the information that bounced back to your brain.

When you *reread* for an assignment, a class discussion, a quiz, or a test, you *anticipate* what will come next, you *decide* what is important to know, you *analyze* (think critically about) that information, and you *record* that information as notes.

Let's Practice!

Pretend your teacher says, "There will be a ten-point quiz tomorrow on how Gandhi used civil disobedience successfully in India."

Go back to Chapter Three and reread the selection on civil disobedience (pages 38–39). After you have finished rereading, can you explain how Gandhi used civil disobedience? You are probably at a loss unless you took some notes! Now check out the following student model. I asked the student to write down his thoughts—in his own words— as they came to him.

READ

I will go back and quickly reread the article in order to be ready for this quiz.

ANTICIPATE

I anticipate that I will have to know about civil disobedience so I need to really read any sentences that have those two words in it.

DECIDE

I need to decide what is important to know about civil disobedience. The quiz will be on how Gandhi used it, so when I see the words civil disobedience, I have to see if it says anything about how Gandhi applied that concept in his country.

ANALYZE

I need to think cirtically and make inferences. It says that civil disobedience doesn't use violence. Gandhi was a lawyer who was discriminated against so he led protests to help people like him. Protests aren't violent but they get people's attention. He got the idea from an American who wrote about it trying to get the government to get out of the Mexican War.

RECORD

I need to write my thinking down. Gandhi was discriminated against by the British and this upset him. He couldn't get a job in India so he moved to South Africa and for 20 years, he protested the British there and got rid of laws against the Indians that said they weren't really married and charged them more taxes. He came back to India and protested for 40 years against the military in India. Hundreds of Indians joined him on a march. He was arrested but was considered a hero for shaking up the Brits.

By using RADAR and writing down his thoughts for the quiz, this student was able to look at some specific ideas on what to read and know for this quiz.

Let's Practice!

Now it's your turn. Pretend your teacher says to you, "Be prepared for a class discussion on what makes Chris Crutcher such a good writer for teens." Reread the selection on author Chris Crutcher in Chapter Three (pages 47–49) and then complete the RADAR notes. Write or type something for all the letters. You don't have to use complete sentences. You may record words, phrases, or fragments—anything that helps you to remember what makes Crutcher a good writer for teens.

Read   Analyze
Anticipate   Record
Decide

REFLECT ON WHAT YOU HAVE LEARNED!

Would you have remembered all you needed to know about why Crutcher makes such a good writer for teens if you hadn't used the RADAR method? Did the RADAR method help you focus your reading? What worked the best for you on the RADAR method? Was it the A in anticipate, the A in analyze, or the R in record, or was it all of them working together?

What if you don't have any direction when you read? What if your teacher doesn't tell you what is going to be on the quiz or test or what you have to know for the class discussion? For example, in the student example and the one you did yourself, the "teacher" told you to know how Gandhi used civil disobedience and what makes Chris Crutcher a good writer for teens. How do you know what to anticipate, decide, analyze, or record if you aren't told?

Tell a Friend!

Another way to help you remember what you read is to write a message or note! That's right! Write a note, an email, or a text to your best friend, your parents, or your teacher telling them about your reading. No one will grade this exercise. It's just a fun way for you to take notes and remember and keep what you read in your head.

In your note, email, or text message:

- State the title and author of what you are reading.
- Briefly summarize what the reading was about. Use the question words as a guide—Who, What, Where, When, Why, and How. They may not all apply. It depends on what kind of reading it is.
- Describe what stood out for you. What was interesting? What did you like or agree with about what you read?
- Tell what you didn't like, disagreed with, or what you confused you. What didn't you understand about the reading?
- Choose three quotes, lines, passages, or events from the reading that you think are important and explain why they are important.

Check out an example on the next page of a text message about John Green's novel, *The Fault in our Stars*!

Sup Neecy!
am reading fault in our stars by john green
it's awes!
takN a br8k to tell u all bout it
It's about this grl who has cancA and she meets and falls in luv
    with a boyo who has cancA 2
de liv in Indy
grl is dying and she meets boyo in a cancA support teen group
the grl is syk and the boyo init
But I think there is se twistD comng nxt
I wndr if boyo will get syk too
My fav parts are when grl Hazel and boyo Augustus learn they love
    the same buk and ritR
wn they vzit the :-X bones at IMA
when they X the 1st time and Hazel fnly agrees to fall in luv evn tho
    she has cancA wn boyo makes her wsh 2fly 2 meet her fav ritR in
    Amsterdam come 2ru
I luv the scen wo de are planning for this wyld trip
the mom is actually kul bout them gng 2gthr
But I dnt get how grl can be so syk and need o2 and still fly
Cnt w8 to read what hpns nxt!
I dnt ever want to get cancA
livN with it swNdz as hrd as dyiN from it
but I hOp I fall in luv with a boyo lk him
read it w/ me plz!
LOL jen

Use this strategy with note writing, email, or online messaging, too. Find a friend who is reading the same thing as you, and exchange texts or emails about the reading. You and your friend can answer each other's questions. By having this virtual discussion, you are studying and keeping what you read in your head.

Let's Practice!

A short story, "A School Ghost Story," follows. Read it and write an email or text message to a friend about what you just read!

English Selection:
"A School Ghost Story" by M. R. James

Introduction to the Story: Two Men Talk
About Being Boys and Their Love of Ghost Stories

Two men are talking about their private school days. "At our school," said A., "we had a ghost's footprint on the staircase."
"What was it like?"
"Oh, very unconvincing. Just the shape of a shoe, with a square toe, if I remember right. The staircase was a stone one. I never heard any story about the thing. That seems odd, when you come to think of it. Why didn't somebody invent one, I wonder?"

A Ghost Story About a Teacher, Mr. Sampson

"Let's see if I can remember the ghost stories from my school. First, there was the house with a room in which a series of people insisted on passing at night; and each of them in the morning was found kneeling in a corner and had just time to say, 'I've seen it,' and died."
"Wasn't that the house in Berkeley Square?"
"I dare say it was. Then there was the man who heard a noise in the passage at night, opened his door, and saw someone crawling toward him on all fours with his eye hanging out on his cheek. There was, besides, let me think—Yes! the room where a man was found dead in bed with a horseshoe mark on his forehead, and the floor under the bed was covered with marks of horseshoes also; I don't know why. Also, there was the lady who, on locking her bedroom door in a strange house, heard a thin voice among the bed curtains say, 'Now we're shut in for the night.' None of those had any explanation or sequel. I wonder if they go on still, those stories."
"From the way in which you said that, I gather that you have."
"I have a ghost story. It happened at my private school thirty-odd years ago, and I haven't any explanation of it.
"The school I mean was near London. It was established in a large and fairly old house—a great white building with very fine grounds about it.

"I came to the school in September, soon after the year 1870; and among the boys who arrived on the same day was one whom I took to: a Highland boy, whom I will call McLeod. I needn't spend time in describing him: the main thing is that I got to know him very well. He was not an exceptional boy in any way—not particularly good at books or games—but he suited me.

"The school was a large one: there must have been from 120 to 130 boys there as a rule, and so a considerable staff of masters was required, and there were rather frequent changes among them.

"One term—perhaps it was my third or fourth—a new master made his appearance. His name was Sampson. He was a tallish, stoutish, pale, black-bearded man. I think we liked him: he had traveled a good deal and had stories that amused us on our school walks, so that there was some competition among us to get within earshot of him. I remember, too—dear me, I have hardly thought of it since then—that he had a charm on his watch chain that attracted my attention one day, and he let me examine it. It was, I now suppose, a gold Byzantine coin; there was an effigy of some absurd emperor on one side; the other side had been worn practically smooth, and he had had cut on it—rather barbarously—his own initials, G.W.S., and a date, 24 July 1865.

"Well, the first odd thing that happened was this. Sampson was doing Latin grammar with us. One of his favourite methods—perhaps it is rather a good one—was to make us construct sentences out of our own heads to illustrate the rules he was trying to make us learn. Now, on this occasion, he was telling us how to express remembering in Latin, and he ordered us each to make a sentence bringing in the verb *memini*, 'I remember.'

"Well, most of us made up some ordinary sentence, such as, 'I remember my father,' or 'He remembers his book,' or something equally uninteresting: and I dare say a good many put down *memino librum meum*, and so forth: but the boy I mentioned—McLeod—was evidently thinking of something more elaborate than that. The rest of us wanted to have our sentences passed and get on to something else, so some kicked him under the desk, and I, who was next to him, poked him and whispered to him to look sharp. But he didn't seem to attend. I looked at his paper and saw he had put down nothing at all. So I jogged him again harder than before and upbraided him sharply for keeping us all waiting. That did have some effect.

"He started and seemed to wake up, and then very quickly he scribbled about a couple of lines on his paper and showed it up with the rest. As it was the last, or nearly the last, to come in, and as

Sampson had a good deal to say to the boys who had written *memini scimus patri meo* and the rest of it, it turned out that the clock struck twelve before he had got to McLeod, and McLeod had to wait afterwards to have his sentence corrected. There was nothing much going on outside when I got out, so I waited for him to come."

Memento putei inter quatuor taxos "Remember . . . "

"He came very slowly when he did arrive, and I guessed there had been some sort of trouble. 'Well,' I said, 'what did you get?' 'Oh, I don't know,' said McLeod, 'nothing much; but I think Sampson's rather sick with me.' 'Why, did you show him up some rot?' 'No fear,' he said. 'It was all right as far as I could see: it was like this: Memento—that's right enough for 'remember,' and it takes a geni-tive,—memento putei inter quatuor taxos.' 'What silly rot!' I said. 'What made you shove that down? What does it mean?' 'That's the funny part,' said McLeod. 'I'm not quite sure what it does mean. All I know is, it just came into my head and I corked it down. I know what I think it means, because just before I wrote it down I had a sort of picture of it in my head. I believe it means 'Remember the well among the four'—what are those dark sort of trees that have red berries on them?'

"'Mountain ashes, I s'pose you mean.' 'I never heard of them,' said McLeod; 'no, I'll tell you—yews.' 'Well, and what did Sampson say?'

"'Why, he was jolly odd about it. When he read it he got up and went to the mantel-piece and stopped quite a long time without saying anything, with his back to me. And then he said, with-out turning round, and rather quiet, 'What do you suppose that means?' I told him what I thought, only I couldn't remember the name of the silly tree; and then he wanted to know why I put it down, and I had to say something or other. And after that, he left off talking about it and asked me how long I'd been here, and where my people lived, and things like that; and then I came away; but he wasn't looking a bit well.'

"I don't remember any more that was said by either of us about this. Next day McLeod took to his bed with a chill or something of the kind, and it was a week or more before he was in school again. And as much as a month went by without anything happening that was noticeable. Whether or not Mr. Sampson was really startled, as McLeod had thought, he didn't show it. I am pretty sure, of course, now, that there was something very curious in his past history, but

I'm not going to pretend that we boys were sharp enough to guess any such thing.

An Extra Paper, Marked in Red

"All the same, I noticed that he hadn't taken any of the papers with him when he ran out. Well, the top paper on the desk was written in red ink—which no one used—and it wasn't in anyone's hand who was in the class. They all looked at it—McLeod and all—and took their dying oaths that it wasn't theirs. Then I thought of counting the bits of paper. And of this I made quite certain: that there were seventeen bits of paper on the desk and sixteen boys in the dorm. Well, I bagged the extra paper and kept it, and I believe I have it now. And now you will want to know what was written on it. It was simple enough and harmless enough: *Si tu non veneris ad me, ego veniam ad te*, which means, I suppose, 'If you don't come to me, I'll come to you.'"

"Could you show me the paper?" interrupted the listener.

"Yes, I could: but there's another odd thing about it. That same afternoon I took it out of my locker—I know for certain it was the same bit, for I made a finger mark on it and no single trace of writing of any kind was there on it. I kept it, as I said, and since that time I have tried various experiments to see whether sympathetic ink had been used, but absolutely without result.

"So much for that. After about half an hour, Sampson looked in again; he said he had felt very unwell and told us we might go. He came rather gingerly to his desk and gave just one look at the uppermost paper; and I suppose he thought he must have been dreaming. Anyhow, he asked no questions.

"That day was a half-holiday, and next day Sampson was in school again, much as usual. That night the third and last incident in my story happened.

A Stranger Visits Sampson in the Night

"We—McLeod and I—slept in a dormitory at right angles to the main building. Sampson slept in the main building on the first floor. There was a very bright full moon. At an hour which I can't tell exactly, but some time between one and two, I was woken up by somebody shaking me. It was McLeod, and a nice state of mind he seemed to be in. 'Come,' he said, 'come, there's a burglar getting in through Sampson's window.' As soon as I could speak, I said, 'Well, why not call out and wake everybody up?' 'No, no,' he said, 'I'm not sure who it is. Don't make a row; come and look.' Naturally I came and looked, and naturally there was no one there. I was cross enough, and should have called McLeod plenty of names; only— I couldn't tell why—it seemed to me that there was something wrong, something that made me very glad I wasn't alone to face it. We were still at the window looking out, and as soon as I could, I asked him what he had heard or seen. 'I didn't hear anything at all,' he said, 'but about five minutes before I woke you, I found myself looking out of this window here, and there was a man sitting or kneeling on Sampson's windowsill and looking in, and I thought he was beckoning.' 'What sort of man?' McLeod wriggled. 'I don't know,' he said, 'but I can tell you one thing—he was beastly thin: and he looked as if he was wet all over, and,' he said, looking round and whispering as if he hardly liked to hear himself, 'I'm not at all sure that he was alive.'

"We went on talking in whispers some time longer and eventually crept back to bed. No one else in the room woke or stirred the whole time. I believe we did sleep a bit afterwards, but we were very cheap next day.

"And next day Mr. Sampson was gone—not to be found—and I believe no trace of him has ever come to light since. In thinking it over, one of the oddest things about it all has seemed to me to be the fact that neither McLeod nor I ever mentioned what we had seen to any third person whatever. Of course no questions were asked on the subject, and if they had been, I am inclined to believe that we could not have made any answer; we seemed unable to speak about it."

Sampson Is Discovered

"Later that same year at a country house in Ireland, my friend was turning over a drawer full of odds and ends in the smoking room. Suddenly he put his hand upon a little box. My friend opened the little box, and found in it a thin gold chain with an object attached to it. He glanced at the object and then took off his spectacles to examine it more narrowly. 'What's the history of this?' he asked. 'Odd enough,' was the answer. 'You know the yew thicket in the shrubbery; well, a year or two back we were cleaning out the old well that used to be in the clearing here, and what do you suppose we found?'"

"Is it possible that you found a body?" said the visitor, with an odd feeling of nervousness.

"We did that; but what's more, in every sense of the word, we found two."

"Good Heavens! Two? Was there anything to show how they got there? Was this thing found with them?"

"It was. Amongst the rags of the clothes that were on one of the bodies. A bad business, whatever the story of it may have been. One body had the arms tight round the other. They must have been there thirty years or more—long enough before we came to this place. You may judge we filled the well up fast enough. Do you make anything of what's cut on that gold coin you have there?"

"I think I can," said my friend, holding it to the light (but he read it without much difficulty); "it seems to be G.W.S., 24 July 1865."

HELPFUL HINTS

One of the best ways you can remember what you read is to question. Questions . . .

- Make us curious
- Make us think
- Make us understand

RAISING QUESTIONS AIDS YOUR READING

Oliver Wendell Holmes, Jr. once said, *"Man's mind, once stretched, never regains its original dimension."*

When you read and question, your reading brain grows, and after it does so, it can't go back. This is a good thing! Think about it. You ask questions all the time. Why does the cat in the hat wear a hat? Why do they call periodic elements periodic? Why is water wet? Why didn't Sarah call last night like she said she would?

There are two types of questions: brainer questions and no brainer questions. No brainer questions require very little thought. The answers to no brainer questions can be found directly in the text. They don't confuse you, and they don't require you to think.

Brainer questions, however, make you think. You must use your background knowledge, infer, look several places in the text to gather information, or perhaps even do further research to answer the question.

Let's Practice!

After you read the following poem, write down or type questions about what you don't understand.

English Selection: "I heard a Fly buzz" by Emily Dickinson

I heard a Fly buzz— when I died—
The Stillness in the Room
Was like the Stillness in the Air—
Between the Heaves of Storm— . . .

I willed my Keepsakes— Signed away
What portion of me be
Assignable— and then it was
There interposed a Fly—

With Blue— uncertain stumbling Buzz—
Between the light— and me—
And then the Windows failed— and then
I could not see to see—

When I read this poem, I have many questions:

- Is she really dying or is this some kind of nightmare?
- Why does she hear a fly and not the other noises surrounding her?
- When the windows fail, does that mean she is dead?
- I wonder what people think about right before they die?
- What is blue?

All these questions are brainer questions. And, they are questions I have because I am curious and because I am confused. If I try to answer these questions myself, I will be forced to reread

Dickinson's poem, and then I will learn more about the poem. If I read it once, I wouldn't be prepared for a quiz, a test, or even a classroom discussion. Check out my answers below.

Q. *Is she really dying or is this some kind of nightmare?*
A. I think she must be really dying because she talks about willing her keepsakes, like signing a will.

Q. *Why does she hear a fly and not the other noises surrounding her?*
A. When I get really quiet and am in deep thought, I sometimes hear things I hadn't heard before. Once when my students were engaged in silent reading and I was reading with them, I kept hearing this "tap, tap, tap." It seemed very loud and was driving me crazy. My school is off a major road but instead of hearing the loud truck traffic, all I could hear was that tapping noise. I looked around and saw it was just one of the students swinging her foot; the plastic on her shoelace was hitting her shoe. It wasn't really loud, but it was all I could hear. She must be used to all the other noises, but the fly buzzing must be different for her.

Q. *When the windows fail, does that mean she is dead?*
A. I think it must be that she is dead because it's like the lights went out. The windows failed means she can't see the windows because she is now in the dark and has passed on.

Q. *I wonder what people think about right before they die?*
A. I have heard about people saying your life passes right before your eyes. I hope I think of my life and family, not a fly.

Q. *What is blue?*
A. I think the blue must mean quiet noise. Like when we think of red, we think loud and fun. The buzz must be a humming kind of noise. I think of how hospitals always have that humming noise because of the equipment. In fact, maybe there isn't a fly at all, it's just that noise and she thinks it is a fly.

Now, my answers may not be exactly right, but my questions are good ones. Because I questioned, I was forced to reread and use Emily Dickinson's words to answer my questions. I can now say I understand the poem better, I would have a lot more to say in class discussion, and I would do well on a pop quiz!

My no brainer questions for the poem would be:

- What is the title of this poem?
- Who is the author?
- What bug is bothering the person?
- What did she will away?
- What failed?

I can answer these without looking at the text or by looking at it very quickly. The title is "I heard a Fly buzz." The author is Emily Dickinson. The bug is a fly. She wills her keepsakes. The windows failed. What am I going to learn from that? Very little! Those questions and answers required no brain power. Remember brainer questions make you think and may have more than one answer.

Let's Practice!

Now, you try. First, read the following poem. Then write five questions and try to answer them. Write questions about anything that confuses you or that you are curious about.

**English Selection: "To J.W.," a poem by Nora Pembroke
(Margaret Moran Dixon McDougall)**

Dear Jane you say you will gather flowers
To win if you may a verse from me
Can you bring to me those brilliant hours
When life was gladdened by poesy?

Bring me the rose with pearls on her breast,
Dropped down as tears from early skies,
Pale lilies gather among the rest
And little daisies, with starry eyes

The heart's-ease bring for many a day
In vain for that flow'ret fair I sought
Turn not your gathering hand away
From the wee blue flower, forget me not

Unless inspiration on them rest
In vain you tempt me to rise and sing
The passage bird that sang in my breast
Has fled away with my life's young spring

My harp on a lonely grave is laid,
Untuned, unstrung, it will lie there long,
If you bring flowers alone dear maid
Without bringing the spirit of song

But accept the friendship that can spring
Out of this romantic heart of mine,
Devoted, true and unwithering,
And for ever thine, for ever thine.

HELPFUL HINTS

As with the texting strategy, you can pair up
with someone—either physically or virtually—to
exchange questions and compare answers. It's a great way
to remember what you read, to study, and to have fun!

Sticky notes

I hate to write in my books—even if I own them. I feel as though I am messing up the pages. So, I use different colors and shapes of sticky notes. My students sometimes use books provided by the school. Because they do not own their books, they are not allowed to write in them. But, in the real world, people write or make notes in their books to help them remember what they read. Sticky notes allow you to write "in" your book. If you are reading online or an electronic textbook, you can add margin notes or virtual sticky notes you can "stick" to your reading.

So that I could allow my students to "write" in their books, I adopted and adapted this strategy from Cris Tovani in her book *I Read It, but I Don't Get It: Comprehension Strategies for Adolescent Readers.*[9] Any time you read something important, you can write your reaction to it on a sticky note. You can record your conversation with the book.

STARTERS

> I already know that …
> This reminds me of …

ASKING QUESTIONS

> I wonder why …?
> Why is it that …?
> What about …?
> What if …?

MAKING CONNECTIONS

> That reminds me of what we
>   studied in …
> This is similar to … because …
> I can relate to that because …
> I agree with this because …
> I disagree with this because …

SUMMARIZING

So, the gist is …

You (the author) are telling me that the most important points to remember are …

- Try to use each prompt once during each reading selection. If you aren't confused about anything or can't agree or disagree with something, write down what someone else might find confusing, agree with, or disagree with instead. The point is that you are stopping and taking notes and rereading more closely and critically.
- When a sentence, a quote, a phrase, a passage, or a paragraph makes you curious about something, makes you question something, or reminds you of something you know about that topic, write that something down on a sticky note and place the sticky note under the words.
- If you are reminded of something like a movie, another story you read, a topic you discussed in another class, something that happened with your family or friends, write that down.
- If you agree with what the author or the character is saying or the character's actions, write down why you agree. Likewise, if you disagree with the author or character, write down why you disagree.
- If you find something that really makes sense to you, or that resonates for you, write down why. If you find something the author or character says that is confusing, write down why it doesn't make sense.
- If you can't get ahold of sticky notes, then just write part of the sentence, quote, or passage and page number on a sheet of paper and stick the paper in the page like a bookmark.

Reread "A School Ghost Story" on pages 97–102. Use all of the sticky note prompts at least once.

STARTERS
I already know that ...
This reminds me of ...

ASKING QUESTIONS
I wonder why ...?
Why is it that ...?
What about ...?
What if ...?

MAKING CONNECTIONS
That reminds me of what we studied in ...
This is similar to ... because ...
I can relate to that because ...
I agree with this because ...
I disagree with this because ...

SUMMARIZING
So, the gist is ...
You (the author) are telling me that the most important
    points to remember are ...

REFLECT ON WHAT YOU HAVE LEARNED!
*Some strategies you learned for keeping what you read
in your head were skimming for information, rereading and
RADAR, rereading and text messaging, rereading and asking
brainer questions, and rereading and using sticky notes.*

Which of these strategies did you find most useful? Which
strategies will you add to your toolbox? Why did they work for
you?

Which strategies did you find confusing? Why didn't they
work for you?

BRAIN TICKLERS
Set # 6

Answer the following multiple-choice questions. Remember to use the strategies discussed in Chapter Two.

1. Skimming for information allows you to quickly locate information you need in a reading selection. Which one of the following strategies is *not* a strategy to use while skimming?
   a. Use the title of the article as a tool.
   b. Use paragraph indentations as a guide to a new idea.
   c. Use the chapter titles as a guide.
   d. Use the boldfaced headings.

2. RADAR stands for **R**ead, **A**nticipate, **D**ecide, **A**nalyze, and **R**ecord. Which one of the following ideas is *not* a benefit of using RADAR?
   a. Some ideas are more important than others.
   b. Using reading RADAR is an effective way to reread and find the important ideas.
   c. RADAR helps you to preview what you will read before you read it.
   d. RADAR allows you to see all the words on the page, but only the information you need is focused in on.

3. Which one of the following statements is true of *only* brainer questions?
   a. Brainer questions can be asked with Who, What, Why, Where, When, and How.
   b. Brainer questions require you to reread and think to find the answers.
   c. Brainer questions are asked by the reader.
   d. Brainer questions must have answers that are long.

(Answers are on page 111.)

BRAIN TICKLERS — THE ANSWERS

Set # 6, page 110

1. **a.** The title won't provide you with any useful information about where to locate the information you need because it just points to the entire selection!

2. **c.** RADAR is for taking notes while you are reading or rereading. It offers no guidance in the before-reading stage.

3. **b.** Choices a, c, and d are true of both brainer and no brainer questions, but only brainer questions force you to reread and think about your questions.

CHAPTER SIX

Different Types of Reading

HOW DO I READ FOR INFORMATION VERSUS READING FOR FUN?

Remember in Chapter Five when I asked if you had ever stayed up late reading a book because you just couldn't put it down? For most of us, that's what pleasure reading is like! Our brain is awake, and we are so into the story that we hang on to every word.

Reading for information

Truthfully, not many of us read textbooks for fun, but that's because they aren't designed for pleasure reading. Like encyclopedias, they are written to provide the reader with facts and information about a topic in, for example, history, science, or math. We couldn't learn without textbooks; that's why you have so many of them! We don't expect you to jump for joy when you are assigned textbook reading. However, once you learn how to

glean information from a textbook, hopefully that kind of reading won't be so difficult in the future.

Reading textbooks requires a special skill set. If you want to learn and you want to do well, you must read. The purpose of this book is to help you help yourself, to help you see that textbooks don't have to be hard to read and that you can even have fun reading them. I love the topic of memoir writing, and I read many textbooks that talk about how to compose memoirs. But, given a choice, I'd rather read a good story any day over a textbook. However, in order to be a good teacher and a good writer, I have to learn as much as I can about literacy.

And the truth is, reading for information is a skill you will need for the rest of your life! Adults need to read for information to survive. For example, adults must read their bills in order to pay them, they must read manuals so they know how to fix the kitchen faucet, they must read contracts to work at their job.

More adults read for information than for pleasure. You will have textbooks in junior high school, high school, college, technical school, and even the military. If you have an after-school job, you will have a job contract with rules and expectations and manuals on how to use equipment. You will have to read and know your driver's education manual in order to drive. Once you are an adult, you will have to read rental agreements, house mortgages, car loans, and even your own kids' textbooks!

I don't mean to overwhelm you, but textbooks aren't going away. As you can see, they might be called something else like a manual, a contract, or an agreement, but it's all the same kind of reading, which is reading for information.

HELPFUL HINTS

Textbooks and other nonfiction or informative reading materials are harder to read than fiction. Remember, fiction is a work that is not true, like a short story or a novel, and nonfiction is a work that is true, like a biography, a textbook, or a manual.

Textbooks don't use characters, plot, or dialogue or any of the other elements of fiction to tell you the information. Textbooks just explain the information. Now, some textbooks may use more illustrations and provide more examples, making them easier to read, but they are still providing information. If you think about it, reading a textbook could be considered easier than reading a story because you don't have to navigate through a "who is who and who did what to whom and where and why" story line. You use your reading brain differently when reading a textbook.

THE TRICK TO READING A TEXTBOOK SUCCESSFULLY IS KNOWING

- How the textbook is set up
- How to break the language code

In order to read successfully, you must be "brainfully fit." That's like physically fit, but with your brain. You must ensure that your brain is warm and that you are actively reading. If you nap through your reading and hope that the information leaps magically into your brain by osmosis, you will learn nothing. Your brain will remain a couch potato.

HOW IS THE TEXTBOOK SET UP?

Knowing how the textbook is set up is like stretching before you run. If you don't stretch, your muscles and body won't get as much out of the run and you will be sore afterwards. In fact, you may never want to run again.

CAUTION—MAJOR MISTAKE TERRITORY!

If you don't take the time to learn how your textbook is set up first, you will waste time trying to figure it out each time you read it. And, you may just give up because it's so frustrating.

When you first receive your textbook, imagine you are an explorer and have just discovered a treasure map that will lead you to a bountiful treasure. Think about and try to find out what all the mysterious marks on the map mean so that you can find the treasure quickly and successfully. The "treasure" is, of course, being able to understand how your textbook is set up.

Textbook Treasure Hunt

When you first receive your textbook, follow these five steps.

Step 1: Title and Author
What is the title of the textbook and who is/are the author(s) or editor(s) of the textbook?

Step 2: Table of Contents
Find the table of contents in the front of the book. How many chapters are there? What is the title of the longest chapter? What is the title of the shortest chapter?

Step 3: Index
Is there an index? (An **index** is an alphabetized list that points out on what page names, places, or topics can be found in the textbook.) Where in the book is the index located? Look up any topic under the letter C and locate it in the textbook.

Step 4: Glossary
Is there a glossary? (A **glossary** is an alphabetized list of words and their meanings. It's like a dictionary that includes just words used in that book.) What page is it on? Look up any word that starts with W. Read the definition.

Step 5: Textbook
What else is in the back of the textbook? Are there any other special sections like maps or lab guidelines or literary elements? If yes, list them and choose one word or one map or one set of guidelines to read.

Let's Practice!

This book is a kind of textbook. Stop right now and take a treasure hunt with this book using the five steps in the Textbook Treasure Hunt.
How did you do?

1. You should have *Painless Reading Comprehension* by Darolyn "Lyn" Jones.
2. There are nine chapters and the longest one is this one— Chapter Six! (It might be hard to tell as Chapters Seven and Three are almost equal length minus a few words.) And the shortest chapter is Chapter Nine.
3. There is an index and it is located in the rear of the book. Under C, you may have found "caricature" which is located in Chapter 4!
4. There is no glossary.
5. Chapter Nine, "Further Reading for Teachers and Parents," is a special section for parents and teachers. Additionally, Chapter Eight, "Books, Books, and More Books," discusses how to find good books to read. It has some interesting subtitles like "Rise Up: Teens Battle Social Injustice" and "Picture this: graphic novels," which lists and discusses good books on those topics.

Choose a different textbook, one you are currently using in a class. If you are struggling with the material in a class, you might want to choose that textbook. Complete the Textbook Treasure Hunt for that book.

Finding the textbook treasure

So, what does working through the five Textbook Treasure Hunt steps mean? What does it tell you about a textbook? Again, let's look at this textbook, *Painless Reading Comprehension*, and think about what our answers mean.

Title and Author. How is the title of the book related to the class you are taking? For example, how does *Painless Reading Comprehension* fit with your class? Perhaps you are using this book in your language arts class or a study skills class or a reading class. Why might your teacher have chosen this book? Probably because the book is about reading and learning about reading in ways that are painless or fun! There is only one author so you know that only one person compiled and wrote the information. Sometimes with multiple authors or editors, the different sections or chapters may not have the same tone or sound the same, depending on who wrote what part.

Table of Contents. Are there many chapters or only a few? The table of contents lets you see how many topics are covered in the book including everything from your reading attitude to using reading organizers. You can also see which chapter has the most information and the least information. You can see ahead of time which topics have more pages devoted to them. You will know right away that you might have to spend more time on those topics in and out of class.

Index. An index points to names, places, and topics covered in the book. If you need to review for a quiz or a test or write a paper and you can't remember where to find information on, for example, Berlin, Sticky Notes, or the Quadratic Equation, you can simply look up the name, place, or topic alphabetically in the index. It will point you to the page or pages where that information can be found.

Glossary. A glossary is handy because, if you need to look up a word while you are reading, you can simply use the glossary instead of going to an outside dictionary source. The glossary is a specialized dictionary with just the words used in the textbook. It won't have all the words, just words the author thinks you might not know. This book does not have a glossary because difficult words are defined with their use in the book.

Reference Section. Finally, knowing what other reference material is available is helpful. Most literature textbooks have a reference section of literary terms. It's a glossary of literary elements complete with examples from the works in the book. Many history textbooks have an atlas or collection of maps that can be used to help you with the geography of historical places and events. Math textbooks might have conversion charts you can look at instead of figuring out the relationships in your head or on paper. Because some teachers and parents will use this book with their students, I included some ideas and help for the teachers and parents.

PREPARING FOR WHAT'S NEXT

Think about a video game. When you play a video game, you have to work your way through each set of obstacles to get to the next level. To be successful at the game, you must know what to expect at each level of the game. Once you have played a few times, for example, you know the one-eyed monster with the green horn and hairy arms will come out in the middle of level two and attempt to destroy you or that the hungry ogre will try to eat you at level four. And, you usually share this information with your friends. Several years ago, a group of my students would converge in my classroom every day prior to our sixth period meeting time and share tips and tricks with each other on how to play a popular video game.

Think of a textbook as a video game. Once you have seen what happens, you are ready for it the next time. You can continue to build civilizations. You can zap out the monster who tries to destroy your hard work. More importantly, though, you can navigate the textbook and find the treasure, which is being a successful reader and learning the information you need.

Now that you have a sense for how the whole textbook is outlined, let's look at specifics. Even though each chapter may be on a different topic, each chapter will be organized the same.

Channeling through the chapter

Choose any chapter in a textbook and channel, travel, or move through it finding the following information so you can see how the chapters are set up.

Goals and Objectives. Are there any goals or objectives listed at the beginning of the chapter? They will probably be listed as statements of fact. If so, list them.

Special Markings. Skim the chapter. Do you see any subheadings in boldface or italics? If so, list them. These subheadings are smaller ideas that are part of the larger ideas. Also, jot down what you know about the topics listed in boldface or italics.

Graphics or Sidebars. Are there any sidebars (boxes with words in them off to the side) or graphics like pictures, charts, or maps in the chapter? Choose one and tell what it says or what it is trying to show.

Exercises. Are there exercises either at the end of each section or at the end of the chapter? Look at the first exercise and at the last exercise. What are they asking you or telling you to do?

Summary. Is there a summary at the end of the chapter or a conclusion? How is it marked? Does it say "conclusion" or "reflection" or something else? Is it in boldface or italics?

Find the five items we just discussed for Chapter Five, "Keeping What You Read in Your Head," of this textbook, **Painless Reading Comprehension**.

Goals and Objectives. The introduction to the chapter explains the problem with keeping what you read in your head, and then the two key methods are listed as:

- Go back and skim for the information you need OR
- Go back, reread, and take notes.

This lets you know that the entire chapter is centered around those two key ideas. And, if you examined all the chapters, you would see that I offer anywhere from two to five key ideas in each chapter that are to be covered.

Special Markings. The subheadings appear on a separate line by themselves, above the text they are discussing. They are: *What Do I Do When I Am Finished Reading?*, *Skimming for Information*, *Rereading Part of the Text*, and *Raising Questions Aids Your Reading*. Titles of the reading selections are set apart from the explanatory text and include **English Selection: "A School Ghost Story" by M. R. James; English Selection: "I heard a Fly buzz" by Emily Dickinson, and English Selection: "To J.W." by Nora Pembroke**. Again, this is true for every chapter. Subheadings and reading selections are set off from the rest of the book with special type.

Graphics or Sidebars. Images are scattered throughout the chapter. I only use artist images in this textbook. The illustrations are usually humorous but are also a visual reminder of the topics. For example, whenever you see an image of a string tied to a finger, be sure to read the passage. It's an important reminder. Some, however, are serious and go along with the reading selections.

Exercises. The exercises are located throughout the chapter under the heading "Let's Practice." The first exercise asks the reader to skim the story on Agnes Vogel. The first question asks: "Where is Agnes Vogel from? What was her life like prior to the war?" The last question asks: "What does Vogel mean when she says the Nazis were 'liquidating the Ghetto'?" In every chapter, each time I tell you about a new way to read, I ask you to practice it as well. I also offer you student models so that you can see firsthand how to do it.

Summary. There is no marked summary or conclusion, just final thoughts in a paragraph at the end of the chapter where I ask you to think about what you have learned in a section called "Reflect on what you have learned." By asking you to reflect, I am asking you to write your own summary. There is also a *Brain Ticklers* section, which quizzes you over key points in the reading.

Let's Practice!

Select any of your current textbooks. Once again, you might choose the textbook for a class in which you are struggling. Channel through the chapter looking for the five items we just discussed.

Knowing how the textbook is set up will save you time and make you a better reader. Each time you go to read your textbook chapter or use the reference sections for an assignment, you won't have to dig through it trying to find the information. You will know what to expect so that you can just concentrate on the idea the words are trying to convey.

Breaking the cryptic code of textbooks

You and your friends have something in common with textbooks. You both have your own set of special words or phrases. Reading a textbook can be like reading an encyclopedia. There is no "Once upon a time . . . ." There aren't usually vivid scene details that help you visualize. Images won't easily pop into your head as they do when you read fiction. You must work harder to create images when you are reading a textbook.

As you have already discovered, a textbook contains thousands of facts, examples, and questions that are broken up into chapters, whereupon those chapters are broken up into sections, and consequently those sections are broken up into words.

How do you take in all of those words and make sense of them? No one would expect you to speak fluent French unless you were French or had been taught how to speak fluent French. The same logic can be applied to textbooks. You need to be taught how to read a textbook. You don't have to learn to speak it or write it, but you do have to learn to read it in order to be a successful reader and learner.

We have seen that the author or editor has already grouped and organized the information in a textbook in a meaningful way. For example, a book on the Civil War is going to be broken down into sections such as causes, battles, and consequences. But, it is still your responsibility to read the information, find the main ideas, and think about what they mean.

To actively read a textbook, you must be alert and awake! No napping or drooling allowed. Think about running a mile. It takes a great deal of effort and stamina. That's how it is when you read a textbook. It's not a short run, and it will take some energy and enduance on your part. But, when it's over, you will feel better because you met a goal and because your body received a workout. The good thing about reading a textbook, though, is you won't have to take a shower and your hair won't be messed up for the rest of the day.

Textbook reading strategies

Stick by the following rules when reading a textbook.

1. If there is a section or chapter summary at the end, read that first! It will tell you the key points to find when you read.
2. Read the information. Don't skim the first time. You don't have to understand every single word, but you do need to read the text in its entirety.
3. While you are reading, pay attention to the vocabulary or the words used in the text. Remember Chapter Four? Use the flag words—such as *so that, as a result of, for example, just as, above all,* and *remember that*—to help you to see how words are put together to create meaning. Also, use the

context around a word to figure out a word's meaning. And if there is a glossary, use that too!

4. Textbooks start out with basic information and then move into more complex and detailed information. After you have read a few paragraphs, stop and think about what you have read. If you don't understand, then go back and reread. Don't go forward; if you aren't getting the more basic information, you won't understand the complex.

5. When you find a main idea or make a connection, jot it down on sticky notes or in your notebook. Remember that taking notes while you read keeps you from napping or drooling.

6. If you see a chart, graph, or picture, stop and "read" it too. Look at it and think about how it fits with the words.

7. There will probably be a summary at the end of the chapter, but not at the end of each section. So, write your own summary for each section. This will help keep your reading and thinking in check.

8. Stop and talk. With a study buddy or friend, stop at the end of each section and talk about what you read. You can use the sticky note prompts to keep your conversation going.

THE SQ3R METHOD

Now that you know the rules, how can the rules be applied? Probably the oldest and most well-known way to read a textbook is a system called SQ3R, which was created by Francis Pleasant Robinson in the 1960s. There are different variations of SQ3R. I modified the SQ3R model we will be using from Robinson's model and used it successfully in my classroom with my students. SQ3R is not a droid! Sorry! SQ3R stands for Survey, Question, Read, Record, and Review.[10]

Survey—Similar to skimming, surveying requires that you get a sense for how the chapter is set up prior to reading it. Read the chapter title, the subheadings, the boldfaced words, the introduction, and the summary. Reading the summary first allows you to see where you are headed; it will introduce you to the big ideas that can guide your reading. It's not like reading the last page of a fiction book or telling the ending to a movie. When I used to teach *Beowulf*, I told my students that both Grendel and Beowulf would die. They needed to read and find out how and why.

Question—Remember when we talked about questions in the last chapter? Use the question words Who, What, Where, When, Why, and How. Turn the chapter title and subheadings into questions using these words and write those questions down. When you read, you then try to find the answers for the questions you created. Again, this gives you a reason to read.

Read the textbook—Read a section at a time. Take breaks in between if necessary.

Record your notes—While you are reading, use the sticky notes or RADAR method we discussed in Chapter Five, the key word notes from Chapter Four, or simply answer the questions you created for the Question part of SQ3R.

Review your notes—Reread your notes and make sure you understand what you read and write.

Let's Practice!

Read the following textbook selection. Survey the selection, question the subheadings, read the selection, record your notes, and review your notes.

Art and English Selection: "Artist Faith Ringgold" by Julie Strawhacker

An Introduction to Faith Ringgold

Faith Ringgold has found much success as an artist, including receiving more than seventy-five awards and seventeen honorary doctorates of fine arts, both National Endowment of the Arts and the Guggenheim fellowships, and having her work in the collections of the New York City Metropolitan Museum of Art, the Museum of Modern Art, and the Studio Museum in Harlem. Today, her work appears in a variety of public places as a result of various com-

missions, some of which include murals that reside in the 125th Street Harlem subway station, a Brooklyn school library, a Women's House of Detention on Riker's Island, and Bronx College, and a quilt in the Crown Heights Public Library. However, Ringgold struggled for many years to find acceptance as an artist in the art community.

Faith Ringgold's Beginnings

Ringgold, who was born on 146th Street in Harlem in 1930, was afflicted with asthma, preventing her from attending school regularly until she was in the second grade. During the many days she spent at home, as a result of her asthma, Ringgold created art with the supplies given to her by her mother. Later, during her senior year in high school, she decided to pursue a career as an artist. She attempted to enroll in the liberal arts program at City University in New York but was informed that, as a woman, her only option was to enroll as a student of education. Ringgold, who came from a family of educators, said the only career you could have as a woman of the South was to be a teacher. Ringgold later graduated from City University in New York with a bachelor's degree in 1955 and a master's degree in 1959, both in education, and taught art in the New York City Public Schools from 1955 to 1973. She said that she considered herself an artist who taught what she loved.

Being a Black Female Artist

Along with teaching, Ringgold painted landscapes in her early career. But, she soon found obstacles to establishing herself as a black female artist. Ringgold later made a statement about male power, and how it relates to women in her story quilt, A Picnic at Giverney in which Willia, Ringgold's alter-ego, sits with a group of clothed feminists in Monet's Garden with a nude Picasso in the corner. In this ironic reversal of Manet's Dejeuner sur l'herbe, Ringgold comments on the portrayal of women in art and the power of the male. She says that men always wear those heavy suits as a symbol of power. At the time Ringgold attempted to take her place as an artist in the New York art community of the early 1960s, she realized that opportunities for minority artists were presented to male, rather than to female, artists. Though determined, Ringgold was not able to find support from the black community, whom she considered to be a group of people that had been cut off from its own artistic culture.

In 1964, Ringgold wrote letters to established black artists, Romare Bearden and Hale Woodruff, in an attempt to join a group of twelve black artists, well-known in the Harlem community. This elite group, which included one female student member, was known as the Spiral Group. Ringgold, however, was not invited to join this male dominated group. But, she didn't give up.

Faith Ringgold: The Activist

In addition to being a black artist and a feminist, Ringgold also became an activist early in her career. In 1959, the year of her graduation from graduate school, she participated in and organized protests and demonstrations against racist policies that were in place in art museums. She made her first contact with other black artists when she joined the Spectrum Gallery in 1966 and participated in the first exhibition of black art there since the 1930s. She also demonstrated in an attempt to persuade the Museum of Modern Art to establish a wing dedicated to Dr. Martin Luther King. The demonstration resulted in the placing of two black people on the board of trustees and the scheduling of two major exhibitions for two male black artists. Ringgold also took part in a demonstration at the Whitney, which resulted in Betye Saar and Barbara Chase-Riboud becoming the first ever black female artists to have their work exhibited there. Today, Ringgold provides fellowship grants to those who study the visual culture of the African American people through her *Anyone Can Fly Foundation*.

In Summary

Ringgold's artistic themes dealing with racial and feminist issues and her desire to address social and political problems were not considered to be a part of the mainstream art of the 1960's and therefore were another roadblock to her gaining recognition as a legitimate artist. The mainstream art of the 1960's was a cool and detached product, not a vehicle for communicating ideas to viewers. Many artists, both black and white, held this as an ideal way to create. The Social Realist style of Faith Ringgold's American People Series and other similar works was seen as being out of touch with the artistic trend of the time.

Survey	Read the section titles. Read the summary first.
Question	Form the section titles into questions.
Read	Read the selection.
Record	Record your notes. Use the sticky note prompts if you would like.

STARTERS
I already know that …
This reminds me of …

ASKING QUESTIONS
I wonder why …?
Why is it that …?
What about …?
What if …?

MAKING CONNECTIONS
That reminds me of what we studied in …
This is similar to … because …
I can relate to that because …
I agree with this because …
I disagree with this because …

Review—Review your notes
How did you do? This isn't an easy piece to read. A student model using SQ3R for the Ringgold reading follows. I asked this student to write down the section titles and the main ideas she read in the summary.

Survey
An Introduction to Faith Ringgold, Faith Ringgold's Beginnings, Being a Black Female Artist, Faith Ringgold: The Activist, and In Summary. The summary tells me that she is going to talk about race, being a woman, and being an artist.

Question

Who is Faith Ringgold? What were Faith Ringgold's beginnings like? Where did she live and work? What is it like to be a black female artist? When was she a black female artist? Why was she an activist? How was she an activist?

Read

I read the selection.

Record

Under each passage below, I put the following sticky notes.

Faith Ringgold has found much success as an artist, including receiving more than seventy-five awards and seventeen honorary doctorates of fine arts.

I know she must be a good artist and very smart to have won all those awards.

However, Ringgold struggled for many years to find acceptance as an artist in the art community.

I wonder why it was so hard for her to become an artist.

She says that men always wear those heavy suits as a symbol of power.

This reminds me of my dad. He calls his business suit the power suit.

Ringgold also took part in a demonstration at the Whitney …

I disagree with protesting if it is violent. As long as it's peaceful like what Martin Luther King did, then it's okay.

Ringgold, however, was not invited to join this male dominated group. But, she didn't give up.

This reminds me of Harriet Tubman, who also never gave up.

TEXTBOOK RESPONSE SHEET

A Textbook Response Sheet is a handy way to break the code because you can read some of the textbook, put it down, and then come back to it later. If you don't have enough time to read a whole chapter but you want to at least get started on the reading or if your teacher gives you some time to read in class but not enough to finish, then using this tool is a good strategy. The Textbook Response Sheet allows you to simply log or jot down notes about what you read so that when you revisit the reading, you can know where you left off. Using the Textbook Response Sheet is similar to what happens at the beginning of a television drama show. Before you get to see today's show, they always say, "Previously on the show…" and then show highlights from the previous show so you can recall what happened and better understand what you are about to watch.

Remember, it's important to think about what you are reading and to take notes while you are reading to keep your brain alert. Textbook reading takes more of your brain power than reading a story.

HELPFUL HINTS

Your Textbook Response Sheet can be set up like this:

1. Chapter title:
2. Pages read today:
3. Subheadings read today:
4. List one important idea learned from each subheading.
5. Write a paragraph (at least five sentences) summarizing what you read today.

Let's Practice!

Read the first five pages of Chapter Four, "Decoding Versus Reading." Look at the student model and see how the student recorded the appropriate information.

TEXTBOOK RESPONSE SHEET

1. Chapter title:
   Decoding Versus Reading
2. Pages read today:
   From 1 to 5
3. Subheadings read today:
   Do You Really Get What You Are Reading? How Do You Connect with the Words? and *Flag words.*
4. List one important idea learned from each subheading.
   Decoding versus reading—Reading is more than just saying and pronouncing the words. You have to understand the text too.
   Making connections—You have to read first in parts and then put it all together to make sense.
   Flag words—Certain words give clues about what is important in the text.

5. Write a paragraph (at least five sentences) summarizing what you read today.

Just because you know how to say a word doesn't mean you know what the word means. Reading means putting all the words and their meanings together to get the message. Words have different meanings depending on how they are used, like the word "heart." It can be an organ in the body. It can also mean courage or a person's innermost emotion.

Let's Practice!

Read the next five pages of Chapter Four and complete the Textbook Response Sheet.

1. Chapter title:
2. Pages read today:
3. Subheadings read today:
4. List one important idea learned from each subheading.
5. Write a paragraph (at least five sentences) summarizing what you read today.

Two-sided notes

Two-Sided Notes are easy, fun, and versatile. You can use them with almost anything and for anything. Simply draw a line lengthwise down the center of a sheet of paper, or use both sides of your notebook pages, or create two columns on your digital device.

CAUTION—MAJOR MISTAKE TERRITORY!

Warning! If you are folding paper, stop after the first fold. Do not continue folding until you have an airplane. You might be tempted to throw it. Your teachers really dislike objects flying around their classrooms, and your notes will be lost in flight.

Now you need to create headings for each side or column. This is easy to do on a sheet of paper or on your computer. Some possible headings for Two-Sided Notes are Subheadings/Facts, Facts/Questions, and Questions/Answers. These three pairs are good to use in a series. As you are reading, jot down the information below.

CHAPTER TITLE HERE

Subheadings/Section	Facts (I learned from reading)

CHAPTER TITLE HERE

Facts (I learned from reading)	Questions (I have about the facts)

CHAPTER TITLE HERE

Questions (I have about the facts)	Answers (What I think they are)

You can use Two-Sided Notes with a whole chapter or just one section.

Another way to organize your Two-Sided Notes is with Cause and Effect. Your social studies or science textbooks will explain historical events or element combinations that clearly follow a cause-and-effect pattern.

CHAPTER TITLE HERE

Cause	Effect

Read the following section, which is from Chapter Three. Complete the three Two-Sided Notes: Subheadings/Facts, Facts/Questions, and Questions/Answers.

Make an inference

An inference is something that is deduced from evidence in the text (like what a detective does). . . . An inference is a reasoning activity. To infer is to reason, to deduce, or to lead to a conclusion.

Inferences are not opinions. Inferences use textual evidence (words and phrases from what you are reading) and personal experiences. When you make an inference or infer, you are using clues from the reading and from your personal connections.

Inferences are not seen text. Seen Text is anything you can see when you read—words, pictures, charts, graphs, and any visual cues that can be used to make meaning—it is what is actually on the page. Inferences are not directly stated by the author. Unseen Text is the information that lives inside your head. Inferences come from inside your head. You have to make them. To infer means to read between the lines. You put together your background knowledge with the author's clues to produce questions that point toward a solution.[11]

CHAPTER THREE: YOUR READING VOICES

Subheadings/Sections	Facts (I learned from reading)
What is an "inference," you ask?	Inferences are drawing conclusions.
	Inferences are not opinions; they use the book.
	Inferences are not seen; you have to think about them.

Facts (I learned from reading)	Questions (I have about the facts)
Inferences are drawing conclusions.	What does it mean to draw a conclusion?
Inferences are not opinions; they use the book.	Can you use both facts and what you think to make an inference?
Inferences are not seen; you have to think about them.	What are you supposed to think about exactly?

CHAPTER THREE: YOUR READING VOICES

Questions (I have about the facts)	Answers
What does it mean to "draw" a conclusion?	You don't actually draw or illustrate, but you come up with or figure out the answer.
Can you use both facts and what you think to make an inference?	You should use both because facts or your thinking alone won't work.
What are you supposed to think about exactly?	You should think about what you know, what you have read, and how you feel about the topic to make an inference.

Let's Practice!

Read the section in Chapter Two titled "Reading Organizers" (page 15) and complete the three Two-Sided Notes or choose a section in a textbook of your choice and complete either all three Two-Sided Notes or just the Cause and Effect one if it applies. Remember that Two-Sided Notes are a way to write down what you are reading, which helps to keep you alert while you are reading and helps you to think about the information you are reading.

Transfiguration

Another fun and useful way to break the cryptic code of text-book language is to change it from textbook language to something more interesting like a poem, a song, a rap, a letter, a newspaper article, or an advertisement. You don't have to be Harry Potter or a superhero to accomplish this feat. You just need your creative brain and crafty writing.

Take a section of a textbook chapter or an entire chapter and rewrite it. Turn those informative words into something fun to read. Not only will you enjoy doing it, but you will learn the information in that section. In order to transfigure it, you need to know what it is you are transfiguring. And, who knows, your teacher may like your version better and use it instead of the textbook!

Let's Practice!

Read the following selection and then check out the rap I wrote.

"The Periodic Table"
by Tom Petersen

Background Information

Everything is made of atoms and when I say everything I mean just about everything. The nails that hold up your house to the plastic case that holds your cell phone are all made of atoms. There are some things smaller than atoms and as logic would dictate they are not made of atoms. (After all how can something smaller than an atom be made of atoms?) But with these few exceptions aside, everything is made of atoms.

1 H																	2 He
3 Li	4 Be											5 B	6 C	7 N	8 O	9 F	10 Ne
11 Na	12 Mg											13 Al	14 Si	15 P	16 S	17 Cl	18 Ar
19 K	20 Ca	21 Sc	22 Ti	23 V	24 Cr	25 Mn	26 Fe	27 Cn	28 Ni	29 Cu	30 Zn	31 Ga	32 Ge	33 As	34 Se	35 Br	36 Kr
37 Rb	38 Sr	39 Y	40 Zr	41 Nb	42 Mo	43 Tc	44 Ru	45 Rh	46 Pd	47 Ag	48 Cd	49 In	50 Sn	51 Sb	52 Te	53 I	54 Xe
55 Cs	56 Ba	57 La	72 Hf	73 Ta	74 W	75 Re	76 Os	77 Ir	78 Pt	79 Au	80 Hg	81 Tl	82 Pb	83 Bi	84 Po	85 At	86 Rn
87 Fr	88 Ra	89 Ac	104 Rf	105 Db	106 Sg	107 Bh	108 Hs	109 Mt	110 Uun	111 Uuu	112 Uub	114 Uuq					

58 Ce	59 Pr	60 Nd	61 Pm	62 Sm	63 Eu	64 Gd	65 Tb	66 Dy	67 Ho	68 Er	69 Tm	70 Yb	71 Lu
90 Th	91 Pa	92 U	93 Np	94 Pu	95 Am	96 Cm	97 Bk	98 Cf	99 Es	100 Fm	101 Md	102 No	103 Lr

Introduction

It should come as no surprise to you that scientists love to collect things. Last year in science you learned about the different plants and animals that scientists have collected. In sixth grade you learned about the different rocks that scientists have collected. In fact, you learned that scientists have used these collections to better understand how things work. For example, scientists place rocks in groups such as sedimentary or metamorphic, etc. Similarly, animals have been placed in groups such as Kingdom and Phylum.

Chemistry is no different. What scientists have been doing the past 200 years is collecting different atoms and grouping them together. This activity has led to the creation of the "Periodic Table of Elements."

Periodic Table of Elements

The periodic table of elements lists all of the different kinds of atoms that have been discovered. Each kind of atom is called an element. For example, element number 1 is a kind of atom called Hydrogen and element number 79 is a kind of atom called Gold. The most up-to-date periodic tables will show that there are 114 different kinds of atoms that have been discovered. Some of these atoms have been discovered within the past ten years and may not be included on older tables. Most tables I come across show at least 110 elements, and for this class that will suit us just fine.

There are a few patterns in the periodic table of which you should be aware. First of all, the elements are arranged according to how heavy they are. Hydrogen (element number one) is the lightest element, while element number 116 is the heaviest. Also, you will notice that there is a zig zag line on the right side of the periodic table. This divides the elements into two groups; metals and nonmetals. The large group of elements on the left of the zig zag line are metals, and they have certain characteristics (or properties) that we associate with metals; specifically, they are shiny, ductile (they can be drawn into wires), malleable (they can be formed into shapes), and they conduct electricity. The elements on the right side are nonmetals, and as the name would imply they are described as not being shiny, ductile, malleable, and they do not conduct electricity. The elements that touch the zig zag line (corners don't count) are called metalloids and they have properties of both metals and nonmetals. There are two exceptions to the metalloid grouping. Even though Aluminum and Polonium touch the zig zag line, they are considered metals.

In addition to numbering and naming each element, you will notice that each element has a symbol. Symbols are either one or two letters long. The first letter is always capitalized. You might also notice that very often, the symbol is a kind of abbreviation for the element name. He is a symbol for Helium and Ne is the symbol for Neon. But sometimes the symbol looks nothing like the name. This is true for Gold, which has the symbol Au, or Sodium, which has the symbol Na. In these cases, the element was discovered long ago before scientists started making the periodic table, and so they used the old name of the element to create the symbol.

The last pattern I would like you to note is the fact that some elements on the table have symbols made of clear letters and others have a solid color. The solid letters are naturally occurring elements. In other words, scientists found these elements already in existence. The elements with the clear letters were created by scientists. They are called synthetic. The larger atoms, for example, are synthetic. (You might be wondering how a scientist would make a big atom. It's a good question but outside the scope of this lesson so suffice it to say that scientists use a device called a nuclear accelerator and smash different atoms together to make bigger atoms.)

"Atoms Are Not Random!" by Darolyn "Lyn" Jones

Atoms are not random;
Everything is made up of Atoms.

Your hi fi, which is so fly,
Is made up of Atoms.

Your Fubu, which is so cool,
Is made up of Atoms.

Your girl, who has your head in a swirl,
She's made up of Atoms.

Because Atoms are not random,
Everything is made up of Atoms.

Because Atoms are not random,
We cannot mishandle the Atoms.

We collect them and store them
In a table, a special and important table.

Poised and proud,
praise the Periodic Table!

The table, so important, is made up of elements.
So relevant because Atoms are not random;
Everything is made up of Atoms.

Organized heavy to light
metal to nonmetal,

No one has to settle.
Because Atoms are not random,
Everything is made up of Atoms.

Atoms have a symbol,
An He for Helium,
An Ne for Neon,
And an Na for Sodium.

Atoms are not random,
Everything is made up of Atoms.

Man made Atoms are clear;
But Natural Atoms are SOLID!

Remember, Atoms are not random,
Everything is made up of Atoms.

You probably have figured out that I do not listen regularly to rap music and am not a good "rhymer." I showed you my rap to prove that if I can do it, you can too. To tell you the truth, I have read that selection many times in the writing of this book, but until I wrote that rap I never really understood what it said. Science is hard for me and to write that rap, I had to reread the selection several times and try to come up with catchy words and phrases to include in my rap. Notice that I only highlight the major ideas and a few details in my rap. But, putting all those ideas and details together creates a summary and an understanding of the periodic table.

Let's Practice!

Take the reading selection on Gandhi from Chapter Three, page 38, and rewrite it as a rap, a poem, or a series of tweets. Remember to pull out the major ideas and details. Look for key words or phrases that you can reuse in your rap, poem, or tweets!

You can also transfigure a textbook reading selection into a story. For example, I could have had the element of Helium, He, tell the story of the periodic table. I could have personified Helium (made him human) and started with "Once upon a time...." Or, I could have asked "He" (Helium) to tell me the story of what happened when the periodic table was formed.

For the Gandhi piece, you could create a Facebook page and then post a series of entries as though you were Gandhi explaining how he came to meet, and then adopt, civil disobedience as his way of leading. You could comment and respond as other individuals from the reading, agreeing and disagreeing.

Or, you can create a "movie" or story trailer. For example, create a story trailer (60- to 90-second clip with sound, images, and words) to try and entice other readers to read the "School Ghost Story" from Chapter Five.

In and out

When you read a textbook, you aren't as involved as when you read for pleasure. You aren't living *in* the character's lives; rather you are taking information *out*. That's part of what makes it harder. It's a two-step process. You need to read the information, let it go into your brain, and then take it out for an assignment, a quiz, or a test. When you read for pleasure, you take it in and let it stay in! You may choose to share your reading or talk about what you are reading with someone else, but there is no pressure to do so. It's nothing formal like an assignment.

REFLECT ON WHAT YOU HAVE LEARNED!

1. Why do you think it is important to understand how a textbook is set up before reading it? What did you find out about how this book is set up that you didn't realize before?

2. Which of the information tips on how to read for information and break the code worked best for you? Why?

3. Which strategies used in this chapter will you use again when reading a textbook, or which tools will you add to your toolbox for textbook reading?

BRAIN TICKLERS
Set # 7

Answer the following multiple-choice questions. Choose the best and most complete answer to the question. Remember to use the strategies outlined earlier and don't look at the answers until you have tried to answer them first!

1. The number one trick to reading a textbook successfully is knowing
   a. How to read a chapter.
   b. How the textbook is set up.
   c. How to speak the textbook language.
   d. How to use Two-Sided Notes.

2. When you first examine a textbook, it's useful to find all of the following sections *except*
   a. The glossary.
   b. The table of contents.
   c. The first chapter.
   d. The index.

3. When you read a chapter of a textbook, pay special attention to
   a. The words, the first page, and the summary.
   b. The goals, special markings such as boldfaced or italicized subtitles, and any graphic images.
   c. The chapter prior to the chapter you are reading, the images, and the last page of summary.
   d. The introduction, the graphics, and the exercises.

(Answers are on page 146.)

BRAIN TICKLERS—THE ANSWERS

Set # 7, page 145

1. **b.** Knowing how to do all the other choices is useful, but by themselves they mean nothing unless you understand the parts of your textbook.

2. **c.** It's not hard nor is it important to locate the first chapter when first investigating how your textbook is set up.

3. **b.** Many of the items listed in the answer choices are useful, but only the combination presented in answer choice b has all the necessary elements.

CHAPTER SEVEN

Reading Strategies

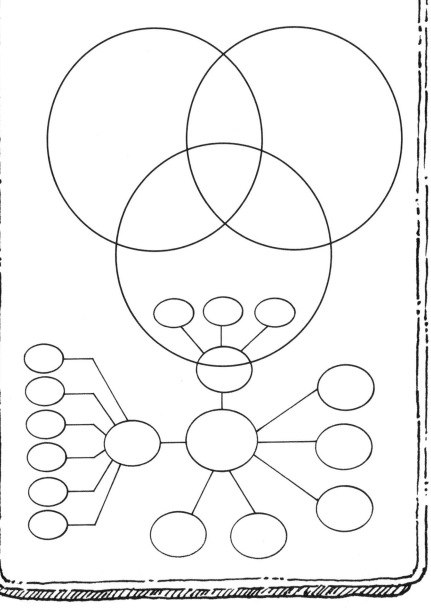

HOW CAN READING AND GRAPHIC ORGANIZERS HELP?

Remember that reading organizers help you organize your reading. Graphic organizers are just what they sound like they are. They are graphics, which are pictures, lines, circles, and other shapes. And, once you add your own words to those shapes, you will have organized your reading. Graphic organizers help guide you, help prompt you, and help you think. They are like glue and help your brain stick to the reading.

BEFORE, DURING, AND AFTER YOU READ

Before you read, reading and graphic organizers remind you of what you already know about a topic and help you to think about what you want or need to know about the topic you will be reading. By asking you to use your background knowledge, you can connect or glue yourself to what you are reading, which makes the reading easier and more interesting.

While you read, graphic organizers help to keep your reading brain alert and awake and focused on what you are reading. They also help you fix up any confusing passages you come across. They may also ask you to predict or think about what is coming next, which again helps to keep you glued to the reading.

After you read, reading and graphic organizers remind you of what you read. They also help you to navigate through all the thousands of words to find the most important ideas in the reading. Finally, they keep what you read in your head.

In this chapter, we are going to practice! You will read passages and try out some more graphic organizers. You will practice using them before you read, while you read, and after you read. You have seen some of the graphic organizers in previous chapters, and a few are new. This is just a practice chapter. You don't have to do every single one. You should always give new ideas a chance, try them out, but if they don't work, then you need to move on. What works for one person may not work for another.

I prefer reading organizers. I like fewer lines and more words because I am not a visual learner. I remember words better than I remember images. But, my friend, Julie, who is an art teacher, loves images. She likes graphic organizers with lots of lines and shapes where she just has to write in a few words. She doesn't mind if the graphic is long and detailed as long as it has lots of images to prompt her thinking.

We all read and think differently. That's what makes us human. The key to being a successful student isn't making A's all the time—it's understanding how you learn and how you read successfully. If you know how you work best and what tools work best for you, then the A's will happen. More importantly, you will know yourself. When you know yourself and how you work, you can conquer anything.

THE 3 DS: DETERMINE, DECIDE, AND DEDUCE

In Chapter Two, we talked about thinking about what you are going to read before you start reading it. We talked about the three Ds: determine, decide, and deduce!

Determine your purpose. Why are you reading this? Answering with "The teacher told me to" doesn't state *your* purpose. Try again. Do you have to memorize the information for a test? Do you have to summarize what you read? Do you have to write a report, explaining the events and motivations? Do you have to make an online poster like Glogster representing symbols about the topic? Do you have to act out a scene? The possibilities are endless. If you aren't sure, then reread the assignment sheet or ask your teacher to clarify. To be successful on the assignment, you need to understand why you are reading it.

Decide what kind of material you are reading. Is it informational—just facts and dates? Is it fiction—a story? Is it a word problem you will have to solve? Is it a process—like how a piece of wood becomes a fossil? Just as we speak in different "languages" in different situations, we read differently depending on what we are reading.

Deduce how much time you will need to do the reading. Deduce or make an educated guess as to how long you will need to do the reading and then add some extra time to that. It may take you longer to read information than to read a fictionalized story or vice versa. Have you ever tried to read a fifteen-page chapter in study hall thirty minutes before it is due? You probably weren't successful. Give yourself plenty of time. Some people need longer than others, and that's okay. There is no award given for speed reading. People who say they can read really fast may be able to, but they may just be decoding and not reading. You know the difference so don't feel pressured to read faster. The reward is that you understand what you have read. Only you know how long it takes you. So, you need to set aside that amount of time and some extra time in case you run into problems. As you read more and practice the techniques in this book, you will discover that you will be able to read faster. But, remember, reading is a process. You have to start at the beginning first.

For each of the practice reading selections in this chapter, I will present you with an "assignment" so that you will know your purpose for reading. And, for each reading selection, you will have two to three graphic organizers with which to practice each of the reading steps: before, during, and after.

PRACTICING WITH READING AND GRAPHIC ORGANIZERS

> **Your Assignment:** Read the following passage on George Washington and explain in a paragraph what role the army, led by Washington, played in founding the United States of America.

Before reading: two-sided notes

Remember that you can organize Two-Sided Notes in a variety of ways. Here I am asking you, before you read the essay on George Washington, to write down what you know about George Washington and what you think about what you know. For example, on the left hand side, I might write down, "George Washington chopped down a cherry tree." And, on the right, I might write down, "I wonder if that is true and if it is, why is that such a big deal to cut down a cherry tree?"

GEORGE WASHINGTON

What facts do I know about George Washington?	What do I think or feel (about what I know about the facts)

Social Studies Selection: "Founding Father George Washington"
by Steve Heiniger

Introduction

Many of our founding fathers deserve credit for initiating independence; however, no other deserves as much credit as George Washington. While many were committing treason by affixing their names to the Declaration of Independence, our first Commander in Chief was placing himself in immediate danger by agreeing to lead the much *maligned* Continental Army. George Washington used his leadership abilities to help the Continental Army survive the season of Revolutionary War and, thus, give the Congressional Congress at Philadelphia the chance to construct the government that would run the newly formed United States of America for now over two hundred years.

The Continental Army versus the British Regulars

The first major engagement between the two main armies came in New York as the British Regulars under command of William Howe with the help of his brother Admiral Howe and a fleet of British warships attempted to reenter independent America and seek revenge for the tremendous loss at Breed's (now referred to as Bunker Hill) Hill where a *scantily* equipped group of make-shift soldiers soundly drove British Forces into retreat until this rag tag army ran out of ammunition and were forced to pack their muskets with rocks and fight hand to hand. The British *retribution* at this later Battle of Long Island is what ultimately convinced George Washington that he would have to simply survive the battles rather than win them in order to be victorious in the war. The British methodic confidence should also be mentioned here as an aid to Washington's great ability to slip away from the British stronghold. It was the consistent way of the British to wait until the next day to finish off the battle that allowed Washington to slip the Continental Army out of New York under the cover of night and fog to fight another day. Although Washington decided to avoid all major conflicts between the two major adversarial armies, he still had to maintain the morale of his soldiers who rarely received pay and always had to fight the elements as well as the enemy because of their lack of funds to pay for proper clothing, shoes, and equipment.

The Crossing

Famous writer Thomas Paine summed up the plight of the army as the "times that try men's souls" as well as the type of soldier needed to participate in this kind of war in his American Crisis papers. Later Washington would have these words read to his remnant of an army that was left at Valley Forge, Pennsylvania.

The overly confident British had just settled into their winter quarters in New York leaving freshly conquered New York in the hands of their rented army from Prussia/Germany known as the Hessians. Washington picked this time for a surprise attack. His victory on Christmas Day carried his troops through the long winter. General Washington committed his troops to crossing the icy Delaware River in the middle of the night as depicted in the famous painting by Emanuel Leutze produced in 1851. This crossing was daring enough, but the troops still had to march to Trenton, New Jersey, in the snow, many of them without shoes, which left a bloody trail that could be easily followed if detected by Hessian scouts. Washington's gamble paid off even after arriving a little later than expected the next morning. The Hessians, who had been partying all night, were caught completely off guard and surrendered, with the Americans not losing a single man in the ensuing battle. Not finished, Washington used another tricky countermove to defeat British regulars who had come to retaliate against the Americans a few days later at Princeton. Washington had correctly counted on the British General hesitating when he arrived. Sure enough, the British waiting to attack the next morning were flanked by American troops who had left fires burning to give the appearance of being camped out, as they moved completely around the British troops. Washington survived yet another year and would soon with the help of his other commanders wear down the British into submission.

Washington's Army Perseveres

In 1777 Washington's army would suffer another defeat, yet another escape as well at the Battle of Brandywine Creek that allowed him to continue the war effort. With a major northern victory and surrender of the British force under General John Burgoyne at Saratoga that convinced the French to side with the Americans the next year, the stage was set for another decision by Washington that would lead to the end of the war. General Washington saw a chance to defeat Cornwallis who commanded the main British force of the South. He abandoned his designs for New York and together with a French force headed south to trap Cornwallis, at Yorktown, Virginia. Arriving early Washington pulled out his old bag of tricks to convince General Cornwallis that the Americans had many more troops than they actually had.

He ordered his men to surround Cornwallis with campfires knowing that this British general would never order his men into battle against a much larger force. This gave other American commanders a chance to bring in their troops and allowed a French fleet of ships time to trap Cornwallis, which eventually brought about an end to the war and led to independence for the United States of America.

Conclusion

George Washington probably wasn't the best field tactician in battle, but did compile a sound strategy of doing just enough in the war to hold his army together and give them the confidence they needed to fight another day. If the Continental Army would have been captured, forced into surrender, or been eliminated due to desertion, America would still most likely have colonial status at best. It is largely due to George Washington's heroics as well as his every day command of his troops that allowed the rest of our founding fathers to create the United States of America.

During reading: vocabulary steps

Create a vocabulary staircase for each of the following three words used in the reading selection on George Washington: *maligned*, *scantily*, and *retribution*.

- Remember that at the first step, you look the word up in the dictionary and write down the first or second definition.
- At the second step, you decide if the definition has a positive connotation, a neutral connotation, or a negative connotation. Recall our discussion of all the different connotations associated with the word *heart*? The word *heart* has a positive connotation because, as we noted earlier, we think of it as one of the most important organs in our body, relate it to having great spirit, or associate it with love. Connotation is the definition and meaning *you* associate with the word. Remember to assign a smiley face to a word that has a positive connotation, a straight face to a word that has a neutral connotation, and a frown to a word that has a negative connotation.
- At the third step, you provide a synonym for the word. A synonym is a word that has the same meaning or nearly the same meaning as the word you are defining. For example, a synonym for *confidant*, who is someone you can tell your secrets to, is *friend*.

- At the fourth step, you offer an antonym for the word. An antonym is a word that has the opposite meaning of the word you are defining. For example, an antonym for the word *confidant* would be *enemy*.
- At the fifth step, you use the word in a sentence.
- The final step, the last step before the top of the staircase, is a fun step. Draw a picture of the word!

After reading: SAM the summarizer

Using the assignment as a guide—*Read the following passage on George Washington and explain in a paragraph what role the army, led by Washington, played in founding the United States of America*—complete the SAM the Summarizer reading organizer by finding important words, phrases, or whole sentences that discuss the role of George Washington and his army on the founding of the United States.

1. Preparing to summarize. Write down your purpose for reading—in other words, your assignment. What are you reading for? What facts, people, events, dates, and so on are you looking for? List the key words from the assignment.
2. Analyze and decide what is important. There are six paragraphs. Put two paragraphs together and come up with important words, explanations, or opinions of the author that help to answer your assignment question.
3. Map it out! Using the author's words, explanations, and opinions and your own words, summarize the answer to the assignment.

Before reading: KWL chart

A KWL chart asks you what you *know* about a topic, what you *want* to know, and what you have *learned*. KWL charts are an effective way to think about what you know and then as you read, jot down questions you might have about the reading. Finally, it allows you to summarize what you have learned after reading. We will use the KWL chart for the before, during, and after reading assignment for the reading selection titled "Commas" by Kim Rowe.

Before you read the lecture on commas, write down or type what you *know* about commas. Write down anything you can think of. Try to write down at least three ideas or more if you can. You might, for example, write, "A comma is used to show a pause."

Before you start reading, write down or type what you *want to know* about commas. Now, please don't say you want to know nothing! Of course, you want to know something. Grammar and mechanics are confusing, and unless you are a trained copy editor, you probably have some problems remembering when you use commas. Again, try to get down at least three questions. You can even think in terms of the rules. For example, I might ask, "Why do some people put a comma before the word 'and' in a list and other people don't? What is the actual rule?" If you are still having problems coming up with what you want to know, then look at some writing. Look at this page or any other page with writing and notice how the commas are used. If you don't know why a comma is used, then write down the sentence and ask why that comma is used! After you have written down three questions, start reading. As you are reading and you come up with other questions, jot those down in the W column.

Finally, when you are finished reading, write down what you have learned. Again, don't write down rules you already knew how to use. Record the new rules or tricks you learned from the reading. Or, explain how, before you started reading, you were confused about a certain rule or use but now, after reading about Mrs. Rowe's piece on commas, you understand.

K—What do I know about commas?	W—What do I want to know or should I know about commas?	L—What have I learned about commas?

English Selection: "Commas"
by Kim Rowe

Commas Are Hard!

Commas are probably one of the most difficult types of punctuation to learn. Once it clicks, you will understand the use of commas the rest of your life. However, getting to the "understanding point" can be a long journey!

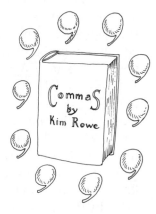

Many adults misuse commas. In fact, just the other day I received an email from a friend that had several comma errors in it. Luckily, this email was only sent to me as a friendly note and not to a boss or an important business client who would expect a more professional, error-free email. More than likely, my friend was writing quickly, and she was not cautious about her grammar. Yet, her errors would have been a big deal if her email was sent to a potential employer; she probably would not receive the job. This is why understanding how to correctly use commas is so important.

Why Use Commas?

Some of my students think that I am crazy when it comes to teaching them about commas. Some of them even call me the "Comma Queen," at least to my face! Maybe it is because I try to drill correct examples into their brains so using commas properly becomes second nature to them. I would like my students to understand how to use commas in a split second—kind of like how quickly Scooby Doo eats a Scooby snack.

One important item to remember is that the sole purpose of using commas is to make sentences easier to understand. A comma tells the reader that he/she should pause when reading, or a comma shows that items should be separated to make the understanding clear.

Let's look at the following example sentence to start:

Example: Mary Ann and Sue went to the store and bought chocolate ice cream vanilla fudge cracker jacks and bread.

Yikes! When reading this sentence without commas, I do not know if two or three people went to the store. Is it Mary Ann or Mary as well as Ann? I also do not know if they bought chocolate and ice cream, or if they bought chocolate ice cream. Did they buy vanilla and fudge or vanilla fudge? The simple use of a few commas would clear up this sentence's meaning.

Example: Mary, Ann, and Sue went to the store and bought chocolate ice cream, vanilla fudge, cracker jacks, and bread.

As mentioned earlier, learning comma usage can be tricky. I try to make learning about commas easy for students. First, I start by helping students realize that practically everyone has misused a comma here and there. Secondly, I try to emphasize that students need to learn the common comma mistakes and learn to not make them.

Another important item is that students should put comma rules immediately into practice. Personally, I think it is pointless for students to memorize the comma rules and be able to recite them word for word. What good is it to know that a comma should be used after two or more introductory prepositional phrases if someone does not even know how to pick out a preposition? It is much more beneficial for students to see an example of how to use the rule in writing. Take, for instance, the following comma rule:

Comma Rule: "Use a comma after two or more introductory prepositional phrases."

Sentence Example: For many years Herb has been vacationing in Cancun.

In this first example sentence there is only one prepositional phrase. According to the rule, no comma is needed. Let's look at a second example where a comma is needed according to the comma rule above.

Sentence Example: After three hours of shopping, Beatrice was ready to go home.

In this sentence we see that there are two prepositional phrases (after three hours and of shopping). This is where a comma is needed.

Common Mistakes

As mentioned earlier, one of the items I emphasize is to learn about the common mistakes people make with commas. Students who know these common errors, and keep them out of their writing, will really improve their writing quality and make fewer errors.

Some common mistakes that people make are placing a comma in a sentence when they think there is a pause, not placing a comma in a comma series, and placing a comma incorrectly when connecting two main clauses. To help you learn more about these common errors, take a look at the following three examples.

Common Error: Placing a comma in a sentence when you think there is a pause.

Rule: There is no rule requiring a comma for a pause in a sentence. Let's look at an example:

Sentence Example Error # 1: Jim needs a break, from mowing the lawn.

Sentence Example Correction: Jim needs a break from mowing the lawn.

Common Error: Not placing a comma in a comma series.

Rule: Use commas when a comma series occurs. Let's look at an example:

Sentence Example Error # 2: Kurt plays basketball, football and soccer.

Sentence Example Correction: Kurt plays basketball, football, and soccer.

Common Error: Placing a comma incorrectly when connecting two main clauses.

Rule: Use a comma to connect two main clauses. Let's look at an example:

Sentence Example Error # 3: This summer Lance is going to Ireland and he is going to visit castles.

Sentence Example Correction: This summer Lance is going to Ireland, and he is going to visit castles.

Comma Tips

Try to think of each comma rule separately. Look at a sentence and try to figure out what rule should be applied. For example, if you do not see introductory prepositional phrases, then you can rule out the two prepositional phrase rule. Basically, fit a rule to a sentence. If students think of commas with an open mind and

have confidence, then they can truly understand comma usage. The
next time you study commas in English class, relax and remember
to break down the rules.

The next two reading selections include a scene titled, "Mama's
Boys, Care Bears, and Fat Girls" by New York playwright Tyler
Dwiggins. This is one of my favorite scenes because it illustrates
two young adults sharing their true attitudes about love and life.
And the next one is a blog titled "Building a Rainbow" by young
adult author Barbara Shoup.

Before reading: Word Write

Before you read the scene from the play, "Mama's Boys, Care
Bears, and Fat Girls," I want you to do some writing. I want you
to think about the words you will run into when you read and
think about what they might mean.

With a Word Write, you choose ten to fifteen words that are
from the first section or if the section is short, such as this one,
from the entire piece. Choose an equal number of words you
do know and words you don't know. Choose nouns like names
and places and verbs that show action. Write the words down
as they appear in the reading. Write a paragraph using any form
of the selected words and in any order you want. Of course, you
can use other words. You would have to do so in order to write a
whole paragraph! Just make sure you use all the words selected.
And don't worry if you use the words incorrectly.

Here is how a Word Write helps you to read. You see the
words standing alone, and then you give them meaning by
writing them down in sentences. Then, after you start reading
the story, play, or piece of nonfiction, you will see the words
again. It is in that second seeing that you will compare how
you used the words to how the author used them. This will
help you to pay closer attention to your reading and keep
you alert during reading!

For this exercise, you will be given ten words from the play
to use. Again, write your own paragraph using all the words
before reading any of the play. Have fun with it! The purpose
of a Word Write is to get your brain thinking about the important
words used in the reading selection. If you don't know what a
word means, guess! Create your own meaning for it.

platonic	adoring
struts	shuffle
flamboyance	unconditional
grungy	breed
illusion	cynical

> **Your Assignment:** Compare and contrast the characters Nate and Roxie in the play, "Mama's Boys, Care Bears, and Fat Girls." Compare and contrast the girl in prison to the author, Barbara Shoup, who is talking with the girl. How are they alike and how are they different?

During reading: Caricature of a Character

One reason why the play or the blog you are about to read might be difficult is that there are different "characters" or people being introduced at various points. Your assignment for both reading selections is to compare and contrast. The play has two fictional characters and the blog has two real people. Both of these reading selections are contemporary, and you should be able to relate to their teen discussions about love and happiness.

While you are reading the play, keep track of the two main fictional characters, Roxie and Nate, and of the two real people, the girl in prison and the author, Barbara. As you hear from each of them and about each of them, write down a description of each character or person. When you describe each one, you need to describe any physical characteristics as well as any mental features, meaning what the character or person is thinking or feeling. Because you may not get all the details you need, you may have to infer meaning or make an educated guess based upon the clues the author presents. For example, in the popular Harry Potter series, we know that Ron has red hair, is short, isn't the best student, and is jealous of Harry. The author always talks about how short Ron is compared to his twin brothers, discusses his red-haired family, shares Ron's feelings of never getting any attention compared to Harry, and reveals how Ron is always asking Hermione for homework help.

If you use your own words to describe the characters or the people in what you are reading, they should begin to make sense to you. You will better understand their motivations and actions or why they say and do what they say and do. After you are finished reading, reread your descriptions and explain how you know what you wrote down. Skim back through the reading and find proof if necessary. Write down words or passages from the story that back up what you think. Use character's words to back up your words! If you need to add more to your descriptions list, do so after you are finished. The Caricature of a Character is a fun and effective tool to use when you must read a story where there are many characters or people and/or when you have an assignment where you need to analyze and write about characters.

For example, for the character of the girl in prison, you might want to draw her wearing "khaki pants, ugly green v-necked shirts, and plastic sandals" because that is what the author, Barbara Shoup, describes her wearing. You could also draw her looking sullen and defiant as she talks about not having anything happy to write about. You know this is an accurate caricature because the author says that she is "scowling" as she explains, "I don't have any happy memories."

CARICATURE OF A CHARACTER

Here are two figures that look like gingerbread men, which you can reproduce on a sheet of paper. You can even draw them any way you want. They can even be stick figures. If you are computer savvy, you can even create an avatar! As you encounter a new character or person in the scene, story, blog, or whatever you are reading, write down the character or person's name above the figure. Then, draw the character's physical features as you see him or her through the author's words. Inside of each of the character's heads, describe the character's personality. Below each figure write down what clues you have that support your descriptions. Find words, phrases, or sentences in the reading that support your description.

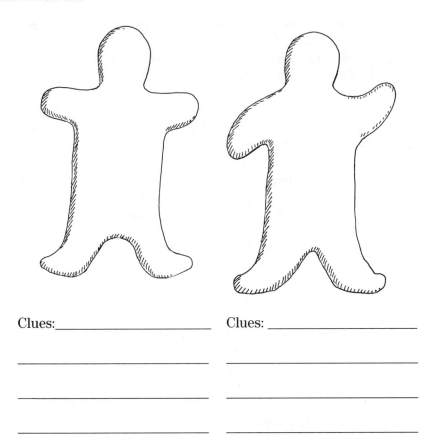

Clues:_____   Clues: _____

_____   _____

_____   _____

_____   _____

A Scene from "Mama's Boys, Care Bears, and Fat Girls"
by Tyler Dwiggins

Enter NATE and ROXIE, who are platonic best friends. They walk on stage and sit on a park bench, watching pedestrians stroll past them. NATE is dressed in an unassuming T-shirt and jeans. ROXIE, as usual, struts like Mick Jagger and dresses with the flamboyance of a lost Spice Girl. A pair of grungy boys roll past on skateboards, ogling Roxie. Roxie notices and winks at them with a megawatt smile on her face.

NATE: Ew, Roxie. What are you doing?

ROXIE: I'm giving them the illusion that they have a shot with me. Call it community service.

(An elderly couple shuffles by, holding hands and looking truly in love.)

NATE: Now, see that's what I want.

ROXIE: You want to have a pair of old people? That can't be legal, Nate.

NATE: No, I mean... I want that completely adoring, unconditional love. The kind of love where you don't care that your husband wears pants so high that they are probably chafing his nipples or that your wife has an afro that looks like she stole the fattest section of a snowman and plopped it on her head.

ROXIE: Yummy?

NATE: No, Rox, seriously. Look at them. Look at the way they shuffle along, holding hands, like they've got all the time in the world. You can tell that they've always loved each other, and they always will. Just that feeling like you can totally be yourself without having to change or keep secrets from one another, you know? Like where you just know they'll never leave.

ROXIE: Oh, Nate... Don't you know? Worrying that you'll lose somebody and trying to keep them around is half the fun. The joy is all in chasing somebody around while trying to look like you're not the one doing the chasing.

NATE: That's not love, Roxie. That's like something on the Discovery Channel.

ROXIE: Oh, *love*, Nate? Really? (She says the word "love" like it's something sour that she has to spit out of her mouth.) Give me a break, Nate. "Love" is for mama's boys, Care Bears, and fat girls to dream of. It's not actually real, Nate. Love is for people who are too afraid to do what mammals are supposed to do, which is find somebody you like the looks of, breed, and move on. Love is not what I'm after.

NATE: That's a smidge cynical, yes?

ROXIE: It's a smidge genius, is what it is.

NATE: But I wuuuv youuu, Roxie. (Nate flings his arms around Roxie and squeezes her into a bear hug. She pretends to be annoyed.)

ROXIE: That is because you are the only good boy left, Nate.

NATE: Not true. But really... I do love you, mi amiga. You know that, right?

ROXIE: I know, doll. I know. Now stop hugging me. You're ruining my image.

"Building a Rainbow" by young adult author Barbara Shoup on her blogspot at http://barbarashoup.blogspot.com/

Black, white, Hispanic, the twenty young women assigned to the Writers' Center of Indiana's third memoir-writing workshop at a prison for girls file into the visiting room for the first session looking wary. They're all dressed exactly the same: khaki pants, ugly green v-necked shirts, plastic sandals. Their hair is poorly cut, their complexions pale from being locked up inside. No makeup is allowed. Some have crudely done tattoos; in some cases, their arms are criss-crossed with small white scars, evidence of cutting. Too many look dazed by the too-high dose of whatever drug some medical bureaucrat prescribed to control them.

The volunteers—writers, teachers, college students—call the names of the girls in their group and the girls go sit down, glancing back at the others still in line. There are six marbled composition books on each table, two each: the one with the "Building a Rainbow" image pasted on front for the writing we'll do in class, the other for the writing they'll do between sessions, on their own.

"These are for us?" at least one girl at each table asks.

They ask it every year and, every year, are astonished when we say yes.

I talk to them about the rainbow image, a scaled down version of the huge poster that hung in my office years ago, when I began teaching. "I grew up in a poor family," I tell them. "My dad drank. My mother was sad. I had big dreams, but I thought whether or not they'd come true was all about being lucky or not being lucky.

"I was confused about happiness, too. I thought it was about how nice your house was, how much your parents didn't have to worry about money, how much stuff you had. I thought it was a state of being. Once happy, you stayed happy, like being in a place.

"But, in fact, you have to make dreams come true," I say. "Look at the rainbow. It's under construction, covered with stick people painting, hammering, working cranes to put things in place.

"And, as for happiness, it's no more than a collection of mostly small moments, strung like beads on a necklace, throughout our lives.

"You can learn how to take the hundreds, maybe thousands of small steps you'll need to take to make your dreams come true; you can learn to recognize and cherish those small moments when you feel right with the world and to build on them until the weight of happy moments is greater than the ones that hurt you and make you sad."

They listen.

They open their "Rainbow" notebooks and, as instructed, write "I remember, I remember," dredging up all kinds of memories— happy and sad. I ask them to pick one happy memory and do the "I Remember" exercise again, dredging up details about that one thing. Willingly, they bend their heads to the task—all but one.

"I don't have any happy memories," she says, scowling.

I go and sit beside her. "None?" I ask.

"None."

"When you were little?"

She shakes her head.

"Toys?" I ask.

"I had a yellow ball."

I ask her to tell me about it.

"It was big. My brother busted it when I was twelve, and all the air went out of it."

But she smiles (for the first time) when she says this. "I loved that ball," she goes on. "I had it from when I was three and my brother was scared I was going to beat him up when I found out."

"But you didn't?"

"Nah," she says. "It was funny he was so scared, though."

I ask if she remembers when she got the ball, and she does. Her uncle bought it for her at Walmart. It was at the top of a tall bin full of balls of all colors and sizes. There were yellow balls closer to the bottom, and her mom said she should just get one of those. But she wanted that yellow ball. Her uncle tried to climb the bin, but it was too rickety. So he went to get an employee to help and, when the man got the ball and held it out to her, her uncle told her to say thank you.

"I ran up and hugged his legs," she says. "I loved my ball so much. It looked like the sun. Yellow is my favorite color, ever since then."

By now, she's talking and writing. Smiling, even laughing at what she remembers. Her mom was wearing a blue dress, her uncle an orange shirt that made him look like a huge tangerine.

Near the end of the class, I ask if anyone would like to read what she's written to the group, and she raises her hand.

So there is one remembered bead for her necklace of happiness: the day she got the yellow ball.

And one, I hope, for the memory of writing about it. There's a bead for my necklace of happiness, too: watching her face change as writing took her back to that happier time; listening as she read her memory aloud; thinking maybe, *maybe* it will make a difference.

After reading: Shape Up Your Reading

The graphic organizer Shape Up Your Reading does just what it sounds like. It helps you size up or give shape to what it is you have read. Below, find a graphic organizer that my teacher education student, Shannon Morris, at Ball State University and I created for you. You can modify or manipulate the directions for each shape as you wish. You can use just one shape or all four. You can use them in any order. For example, you can start with the square, the circle, or the star! For example, for the star, you can find one important idea or five. This is a super way to summarize and rethink what you read so you can keep it in your head. Complete the Shape Up Your Reading with the blog in this chapter titled, "Building a Rainbow."[12]

The Star
Write down the five most important ideas, topics, events, or themes from your reading in each star point.

The Triangle
Write down three supporting ideas from the reading on each leg that support a star point.

Circle

Write down any recurring problem or question that keeps coming up in your reading. Wrap and write your question all the way around the circle.

Square

On each side, write down any four background or building block pieces of information that might help solve the recurring problem or question. What do you know and what does the reading say about your question? Suggestion: Use your supporting ideas from the triangle to help you.

Wow! Using those organizers are fun, isn't it? Did you notice the words you had to write about in the Word Write pop up more while you read the play? Were you looking for them? What does "platonic" mean, anyway? The Caricature of a Character and Shape Up Your Reading can be a lot of work, but when you write about something using your own words, and then you look for the author's words, your brain automatically pays closer attention. Your reading selections were not easy to read, but after you did all of that, it should have been much easier.

Your Assignment: For this reading selection on greatest common factors, you will be practicing SQ3R. Remember that SQ3R stands for Survey, Question, Read, Record, and Review.

Before, during, and after reading: SQ3R

The next reading selection is about math. Now, those may sound like contradictory terms, but they aren't! Math isn't just numbers. In order to understand the numbers in math problems, you first need to read about them. In fact, reading math can be harder because you must read words, symbols, and numbers!

In every math lesson, there is a one- to two-page written explanation about that lesson. In every story problem, there are words, and you need to translate the words into numbers and the numbers into a problem. So, knowing how to "read" math is very important.

Surveying is similar to skimming. Surveying requires you to get a sense of how the chapter or reading selection is set up prior to reading it. Read the title, any subheadings, the boldfaced words, the introduction, and the summary if there is one. Reading the summary first allows you to see where you are headed—the big ideas that can guide your reading.

To question, use the question words Who, What, Where, When, Why, and How. Turn the chapter title and subheadings into questions using the question words. Then when you read, you can try to find the answers to the questions you created.

Finally, read the selection. Read a section at a time. Take breaks in between if you need to.

Record your notes. While you are reading, answer the questions you created for the question section of SQ3R.

Finally, review your notes. Reread your notes and make sure you understand what you read and write.

SQ3R is not only an effective way to read a difficult passage but also a super way to study for a quiz. Watching the teacher solve problems on **Greatest Common Factor** and knowing how to solve them yourself is only half the equation. To really understand math concepts, you must understand the terms and the explanation of why and how such ideas like greatest common factor exist.

Survey—Read the title, any subheadings, the boldfaced words, the introduction, and the summary if there is one.

Question—Take the subtitles and words in boldfaced type and create questions using each of the question words.

Who?

What?

Why?

Where?

When?

How?

Read the selection written by Mrs. Forkner.

Record your notes—Write down answers to your questions above.

Review your notes—Reread your questions and answers and maybe even resolve the problems to make sure you understand.

"Greatest Common Factor"
by Deb Forkner

Introduction: Definitions to Know

Look at each word: "greatest" means largest.

"Common" means something alike. If you and I have eye color in common, it means we both have brown eyes.

"Factor" means to multiply with another number to give the desired product. For example, the factors of 6 are 1, 2, 3, and 6. $1 \times 6 = 6$, $2 \times 3 = 6$. So, GCF is the largest factor 2 numbers have alike.

Strategies for Finding the GCF: The List Method

One method for finding GCF is the list method. If we want to find the GCF of 12 and 20, we would start by listing all the factors of 12 and listing all the factors of 20.

12: 1, 2, 3, 4, 6, 12

20: 1, 2, 4, 5, 10, 20

So, by examining the lists of factors you can see that 4 is the largest factor that is in both lists. So 4 is the largest factor that 12 and 20 have in common. 4 is the GCF of 12 and 20.

Strategies for Finding the GCF: Prime Factorization

Now, let's use the same numbers, 12 and 20, but do the prime factorization method.

First, get the prime factorization of 12 and 20. Then we will compare their prime factors.

| 12 | 2 × | 2 × | 3 |
| 20 | 2 × | 2 × | 5 |

$$GCF = 2 \times 2 = 4$$

Look carefully at the prime factorizations. Each has 2 • 2 = 4. So like the list method, we get the same GCF of 4.

Let's try 2 more numbers and use the prime factorization method only.

Try finding the GCF of 42 and 105.

The prime factorization of 42 is 2 • 3 • 7

The prime factorization of 105 is 3 • 5 • 7

| 42 | 2 × | 3 × | 7 |
| 105 | 5 × | 3 × | 7 |

$$GCF = 3 \times 7 = 21$$

They have in common a factor of 3 and a factor of 7.

So the product of the factors they have in common is 21; 21 is the GCF of 42 and 105.

Let's Practice: Finding the GCF

Find the GCF of 25 and 32.

The prime factorization of 25 is 5 • 5.

The prime factorization of 32 is 2 • 2 • 2 • 2 • 2.

What factor(s) do 25 and 32 have in common? Before you answer, go back and list all the factors of 25 and 32,

25: 1, 5, 25

32: 1, 2, 4, 8, 16, 32

25	5 ×	5				
32		2 ×	2 ×	2 ×	2 ×	2

$$GCF = 1$$

You can see from the lists of factors that 25 and 32 have a GCF of 1. When that occurs, the two numbers are called relatively prime. Neither number is prime, but when the greatest common factor is one, they are considered relatively prime numbers. One is a factor of all numbers.

Summary

GCF stands for *greatest common factor*. Remember that the GCF is the product of the common primes. Something that is prime is a positive integer that has exactly two positive integer factors, 1 and itself. If we list the factors of 24, we have 1, 2, 3, 4, 6, 8, 12, and 24. That's eight factors. If we list the factors of 11, we only have 1 and 11. That's 2. So we say that 11 is a prime number, but 24 isn't. There are two methods in finding the GCF which are The List Method and Prime Factorization.

REFLECT ON WHAT YOU HAVE LEARNED!

If we just sit down and don't take the time to think about what we are going to read before we read it and keep our brain active while we are reading it, it's hard to do anything after! Reading organizers may seem like a lot of work, but if you take the time to do them before and during reading, they make your homework easier once you have finished reading—and you actually understand what you read.

Which reading organizers work well for you? Which ones will you add to your toolbox?

BRAIN TICKLERS
Set # 8

Remember, to master the multiple-choice questions, use the strategies learned in Chapter Two!

1. When you use the vocabulary staircase, you assign words a face with a smile, a face with a frown, or a straight face based upon the word's connotation. What is the connotation of a word?
   a. Part of speech
   b. Dictionary definition
   c. Definition you associate with the word
   d. Denotation of a word

2. What is the point of using the Word Write and writing a paragraph and making up meanings for words you don't know?
   a. Seeing the words and using the words helps your brain warm up to the words.
   b. Seeing the words helps you to look them up in the dictionary.
   c. Seeing the words helps you to write the paragraph.
   d. Seeing the words helps explain the paragraph.

3. When you complete a Caricature of a Character, you write down not only what he/she looks like but what he/she is thinking as well. What if the character doesn't say what he/she is thinking or feeling? What do you do?
   a. You leave it blank.
   b. You guess.
   c. You write down what you are feeling or thinking.
   d. You infer what the character is thinking or feeling.

(Answers are on page 176.)

BRAIN TICKLERS—THE ANSWERS

Set # 8, page 175

1. **c.** Remember that denotation is the dictionary definition of a word and connotation is the meaning we associate with a word.

2. **a.** The research says that we have to see a word as many as fifteen times before we know it. The more exposure we have to a word, such as seeing it in a Word Write, writing it, and then encountering it later in reading means we have a greater chance of remembering that word.

3. **d.** The author most likely will not say exactly so it is up to us, the reader, to read between the lines and gather evidence so we can know the characters.

CHAPTER EIGHT

Books, Books, and More Books

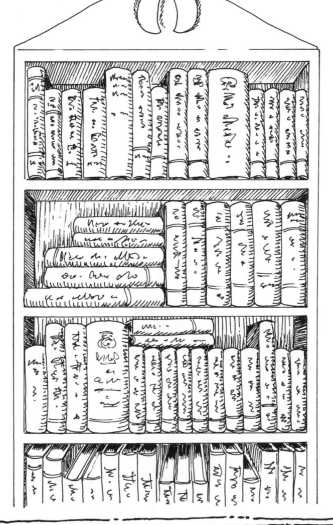

I CAN'T FIND A GOOD BOOK TO READ!

The book publishing world is on fire these days. More books are being published than ever before, which means you have more books to choose from than your grandparents or parents ever had when they were your age. And now you can read them in print or electronically.

Remember in Chapter One when I asked you what your favorite book memory was? What was your favorite picture book when you were young?

Name a book you have read within the last two years that you would say is your favorite.

My latest favorite book is *Fever 1793* by Laurie Halse Anderson. I love history, and this book is a fiction tale of a real event, the yellow fever that hit Philadelphia in 1793 and wiped out ten percent of the city's population, over 5,000 people in just three months. The main character, Mattie Cook, is a typical teenage girl. She thinks her mother is old fashioned, a boy down the street is cute, and that working every day is a real bore. But, when the fever comes and her family and friends begin to get sick and die, Mattie has to learn to survive and take care of the business and her family. Mattie writes about her experiences in diary format which makes it fun and interesting to read. I got lost in the story while learning history—what a deal!

REFLECT ON WHAT YOU DO!

How and where do you find good books to read?

Does that work well for you? Are you happy with the choices?

How do I find a good book to read?

If you don't have any ideas about how and where to find a good book to read or your methods haven't worked with much success, just keep reading. One of these methods will work for you!

Talk to your friends

First, talk to your friends. If you and your friends like the same things, chances are you will like to read the same books. That's how most of us hear about good books. Our friends talk to us about a good book they just finished and tell us we just have to read it! Ask your friends what they are reading and check out the book. It might be one you want to read as well.

Check out an author or topic

Another way to find a good book is to check out an author. If you liked a book by a certain author, chances are you would like another book he or she has written. I know that many of my students love author Gary Paulsen and read all of his books. Many students read *Hatchet* first and then read more of his books, like *Brian's Winter* or *Guts*.

You may just like a certain topic. For example, Gary Paulsen's *Hatchet* is a survival and wilderness tale. If you liked reading about survival in the wilderness, you may want to check out other books that are on the same topic like Ben Mikaelsen's *Rescue Josh McGuire*.

Visit a library or bookstore or go online

Take a walk through the library or bookstore, or search an online site. The search can be overwhelming because there are so many books! You start this adventure with the librarian or teacher or a bookstore worker. Approach that person and tell him or her that you need help finding some good books to read. If you go online, do a search with words or phrases that describe your interests, such as, "teen vampire" or "football stories" or "World War II." You can read the summary and other readers' reviews to help you as well.

If you aren't directed to some good books or you don't want to ask, then you will have to browse. Browsing is actually my favorite. I love looking at the book covers and reading the flaps to see if this lonely book sitting on the shelf could turn out to be a wonderful tale.

HELPFUL HINTS

Tips for Browsing

- Decide on a genre. Do you like fiction, nonfiction, or perhaps biographies? Most libraries will have the fiction arranged alphabetically by the author's last name, and nonfiction arranged by the Dewey Decimal system, and the biographies arranged alphabetically by the individual the story is about. Decide which genre you are most interested in and head to that section.
- Move up and down the aisles, or through the Internet pages, stopping periodically to look at the book covers. If the cover art appeals to you, then read the title. Is it an interesting title? Does it catch your attention? For example, I checked out a children's book because the title, *Walter the Farting Dog,* sounded really funny and I like dogs.
- Read the back of the book or the flap, which often has a quick summary or reviews.
- Flip through the pages and look at the print. Does it look like something you can read with ease?
- Read the first page. Does it make you want to continue reading?
- Check out the table of contents. Is it broken into chapters or sections?
- If after looking at the art, the title, the print, the summary, the first page, and the table of contents, you are sold—then get it! If not, keep on browsing. Get more than one book in case you don't like one as well as you thought you would or if one turns out to be too hard to read. I always tell my students to give a book ten pages. If after reading ten pages you aren't hooked, then forget it and start reading something else.

Use the web

A final suggestion for finding good books is to use the web! I use the Internet often, accessing it from my phone and laptop. I look up books and book reviews online before I head to the library or bookstore so I have some ideas as to what I want to look for or buy. Below are some of my student's favorite teen book web sites. Every site listed below includes all the different genres— from graphic novels to fantasy series to historical fiction and everything in between.

- **Reading Rants: Out of the Ordinary Teen Book Lists**—*http://www.readingrants.org* This web site, compiled by a school librarian, offers racy reviews by teens of what teens are really reading!
- **Teen Reads**—*www.teenreads.com* This web site includes news and feature articles about books, authors, and pop culture.
- **Young Adult Library Services Association (YALSA)**—*http://www.ala.org/yalsa/booklistsawards/booklistsbook.cfm* This American Library Association (ALA) web site highlights the teen award winners and voted best teen picks by year.
- **Young Adult Reads**—*http://www.yareads.com*—This web site offers teen book reviews written by and for teens. The reviews are monitored and can be submitted on a forum using multiple social networking tools.

BOOKS THAT INTEREST TEENS

I have compiled a list of the top three books recommended to me by students your age in a number of different categories. Over the years, I have had countless students say to me, "Mrs. Jones, I had never read an entire book all the way through until I read this book. You have to read it!" Or, "Mrs. Jones, thanks for recommending this book to me. It's the best book I have ever read!"

Now, I am not trying to "toot my own horn." But of all my responsibilities as a teacher, the one I take the greatest joy in is connecting kids to books. When one of my students tells me that he or she hates to read or has never read a book all the way through, I see it as a challenge. I am determined to find a book for that student. I believe everyone who claims to hate to read just hasn't found his or her book yet.

The lists of books that follow are based upon genre and topic. For example, under "Rise Up: Teens Battle Social Injustice," I have compiled books that students would pass around as "must reads." So, browse through my lists, jot down some titles, and head to your local library or bookstore and check them out! Under "History Buff," I have shared top books based upon history topics typically discussed in middle school or junior high school. Under "Picture This: Graphic Novels," I have compiled favorite comic book–style novels. If you are a comic book or Manga reader, check these out—they are wonderful to look at and to read.

I have rated the books as easy read, average read, and complex read. Please note that even the books that I list as a complex read are so good that most of my students who didn't even consider themselves good readers took them on anyway. It may have taken them a little longer, but they all said it was worth it!

"Rise Up: Teens Battle Social Injustice"

Speak by Laurie Halse Anderson is the story of Melinda, who is date raped by a high school boy she has a crush on. After the terrible events of the evening, when no one else will help her, Melinda stops speaking. She only speaks through her thoughts, which you read, and through her art, which she creates. Find out how her art speaks and how she finally finds her voice to tell the truth. This average read highlights the freshman difficulties of dealing with cruel gossip, rape, and pain.

Esperanza Rising by Pam Munoz Ryan details the life of Esperanza, who lives a very privileged life in Mexico. When her father is killed and her home and land taken away, Esperanza must come to America and work as a migrant worker. She and her mother face death, hardship, and starvation, but she lives up to her name, Esperanza, which means hope, and thrives. This average read is filled with history, culture, love, and hope.

Yaqui Delgado Wants to Kick Your Ass by Meg Medina is the story of Piddy Sanchez who is bullied by a girl named Yaqui and her group at school. Piddy doesn't even know who she is, but Yaqui decides she hates her and makes her a target both in and out of school because she doesn't think Piddy is Latin enough. Piddy has just moved with her mother to a new neighborhood and school, and she hates it. She has no friends and only enemies. Piddy starts to fail in school and her dreams of becoming a scientist fall away. Too afraid to tell her mother about the harassment, she begins to fight with her mother and lose everything she has worked so hard for, to be the first in her family to go to college. But, read and learn how this heroine Piddy survives in this complex and dark read.

"Facing and Overcoming Despair and Death"

Touching Spirit Bear by Ben Mikaelsen is the story of Cole Matthews. Cole has a terrible home life and a history of violence. When he nearly beats a student to death, he is offered "circle justice" before jail. He becomes part of a real custom of the Tlinget Native Americans of sending the accused to live off the land of a remote island for a year. Read about Cole's near death and survival on the island and how he learns to live again as a better person. This easy read is action-packed.

Holes by Louis Sachar is so popular that it has been made into a movie. The book is better. Stanley Yelnets has to dig a five-foot hole every day as part of his punishment at a youth detention center named Camp Green Lake. Yellow-spotted lizards, bad food, intense heat, and a warden looking for fortune gave Stanley plenty of reasons to give up on life. Stanley toughened up and toughed it out. In the process, he discovered that curse or no curse, you have to make your own luck. This average read is filled with fantasy, humor, and action.

Monster by Walter Dean Myers is the name the prosecutor gives the main character, Steve. Steve claims he was in the wrong place at the wrong time when a convenience store worker got shot. Steve wants to be a filmmaker, so to keep his mind and nerves calm during the trial, he records the events of the trial as if they are appearing in a movie script. The reader then becomes the jury as you enter into Steve's world. This average read is written in teen speak and is an intense book.

History Buff

My Brother Sam Is Dead by James Lincoln Collier and Christopher Collier is told by young Tim, whose family is torn apart by the Revolutionary War. His father supports the British, while his teenage brother goes to fight with the Revolutionaries. This story has many twists and turns, and the ending is surprising. The events in the story are real, and the family is based on an actual family. This is an average read, and you will learn about the sacrifices people made to establish our great country.

Out of the Dust by Karen Hesse is an incredible story of fourteen-year-old Billie Jo, who lives in the Oklahoma dustbowl during the American Depression. The constant poverty, hard life, and storms take their toll on Billie Jo and her family. Her mother dies, her father is dying, and her beloved piano is swept away in the dust, and her hands that once loved to play are damaged in a fire. Billie Jo turns that dust into grit and runs away and leaves that life behind. The novel is written in a poetic fashion and is easy to read and leaves the reader with a better understanding of what hope looks like.

Soldier's Heart: Being the Story of the Enlistment and Due Service of the Boy Charley Goddard in the First Minnesota Volunteers by Gary Paulsen is a fiction tale based on a real person, Charley Goddard, and his life as a young Civil War soldier. This book is beloved by both girls and boys. Charley is young and naïve and full of war glory when he lies about his age and joins the war. After almost starving to death, watching his friends die, and stacking dead bodies up to shield himself from the cold, Charley learns how terrible war is. This historically accurate and easy read is eventful and shows the whole truth about war.

Fantastic Fantasy Tales

The Hobbit: or There and Back Again by J.R.R. Tolkien is a timeless fantasy tale that sets up the *Lord of the Rings* trilogy. The main character, Bilbo Baggins, lives a good life in the shire but dreams of adventure. With his wizard friend Gandalf, they encounter amazing creatures, danger, and awe-inspiring magic. Bilbo wins a ring in a contest, which changes him and will change you when you read this tale. This average read can sometimes have some difficult vocabulary, but the action and characters will keep you easily moving through. Most students are familiar with the *Lord of the Rings* trilogy or the movie, but I recommend you read the book that started it all.

The Hero and the Crown by Robin McKinley is a Newbery Medal award winner and classic, timeless piece. The main character, Princess Aerin, has a father who is a king and a mother who is a witch. The people of her village think her mother is evil. Aerin is torn and uncertain of her future, but a blue sword changes her. I do not like to read fantasy, but I loved this book. My students agreed, as it can be a complex read but is packed with "spellbinding" action and a strong group of young adult characters.

The Forestwife by Theresa Tomlinson is an easy-to-read, short, and fascinating fantasy story that is based on actual history and legend intertwined with magic and myth. The main character is Lady Marian from *Robin Hood*. Unlike the story of Robin Hood, we learn in this story that it is Lady or Maid Marian who chooses to live in the forest with the forest people and become their heroine. She and her band of women come together to survive and fight oppression against the tyranny surrounding them. Since the last edition of this book, two sequels have been added, titled *Child of May* and *In The Path of the She Wolf*.

Popular Series Read

The *Crank* Series by Ellen Hopkins includes *Crank, Glass*, and *Fallout* and is a series about a young woman named Kristina who becomes addicted to "the monster" (crystal meth) and while on the drug, she turns into someone different who in her mind is better than who she is. She becomes more and more addicted and eventually becomes pregnant. She decides to keep the child and in the second book, *Glass*, she has the baby but remains addicted and her mother kicks her out and keeps the baby. Kristina spirals further and further down and in the third book, *Fallout*, she has five children and the story focuses on her children and their relatives and how they survive with and without Kristina. Hopkins writes each page like a piece of poetry, and while this average read series often includes mature young adult content, the series highlights the very serious topic of drug addiction among young adults and the consequences of those choices, and it is hard to put down.

The Hunger Games Trilogy by Suzanne Collins is comprised of three titles: *The Hunger Games, Catching Fire*, and *Mockingjay*. In the dystopian nation of Panem, one boy and one girl from each district are chosen to participate in the Hunger Games where they are forced to fight to the death on television. Katniss' sister is chosen, and Katniss herself becomes a contender to save her sister's life. Learn if and how she survives and what happens when Katniss fights President Snow and his district to improve the lives of the people in this average and exciting trilogy read!

The *Harry Potter* Series by J.K. Rowling includes *Harry Potter and the Sorcerer's Stone, Harry Potter and the Chamber of Secrets, Harry Potter and the Prisoner of Azkaban, Harry Potter and the Goblet of Fire, Harry Potter and the Order of the Phoenix, Harry Potter and the Half-Blood Prince*, and *Harry Potter and the Deathly Hallows*. I had to keep this in this new edition because if you haven't read any *Harry Potter* books, you will love them. I have seen kids who have never read a book read all seven. The *Harry Potter* books are not just good but great books to read and reread. The series chronicles the story of boy wizard Harry, who is born from very famous wizarding parents who die at the hand of a dark lord, Valdemort. Harry is raised by his often cruel aunt and uncle who are Muggles, not wizards. He is born a wanted wizard and once he enters the Hogwart's school, his life becomes about keeping himself and his friends alive against Valdemort. If you have only seen the movies, you are missing out. This easy-to-read and action-packed series is hard to put down. Even though the setting is magical, the problems encountered by young adults and then teens Harry and his friends are relevant to this world.

Picture This: Graphic Novels

American Born Chinese by Gene Luen Yang is the story of middle school student, Jin Wang, who spins three different story lines and then brings them all together at the end. The first story is about his lonely and difficult life of assimilating as an Asian-American student in a predominantly white school. The second story is about an American white student named Danny. The third story is about Jin Wang's dream of being the Monkey King, a cultural icon in Kung Fu. Each has their own personal story and all are part of Jin Wang, and they all come colliding together in the most amazing way. Each learns the meaning of each story and event that takes place. This action-packed and remarkably illustrated graphic novel is an easy, entertaining, and enlightening read.

The Complete Maus by Art Spiegelman is a graphic novel about the Holocaust. The author's father was a Holocaust survivor and the book shares his experiences as told to his son. In this book, the Nazis are depicted as cats, the Jews as mice, and the American soldiers as dogs. This complex read was a favorite of my students because of the way the art helped explain a difficult topic.

Pedro and Me by Judd Winick is about the friendship of Pedro Zamora and Judd Winick, both early contestants on the MTV show *Real World*. Pedro had AIDS and was compelled to educate other teens about his disease. Judd, a cartoonist, celebrated Pedro's life and message through this graphic novel. This is an easy-to-read book and is a favorite among all young people, as its topic talks about real issues facing teens who are different.

"Take me out to the ball game!" Popular Sports Novels

Whale Talk by Chris Crutcher is about TJ, a high school senior who is black, Japanese, and white. He is an outstanding athlete but is sick of the jocks' attitude and decides to create his own swim team, made up of non-athletes. TJ discovers who his real friends are, who he is, and what it means to be a leader. Check out this average read if you like reading about swimmers, if you know what it's like to be torn between two worlds, or if you have ever felt like doing something drastic because you are sick of playing by the rules.

The Contender by Robert Lipsyte is a classic young adult novel about a high school dropout named Alfred. His friends are into drugs. He is into nothing. The street life is getting to him. He visits a neighborhood gym and boxing club, and it changes his life. He learns to fight—on the streets, in the ring, and for himself. He finds his calling. I have yet to have a young man who doesn't like this average read, classic book.

Hoops by Walter Dean Myers is the story of a star basketball player, Lonnie, who becomes friends with a former professional basketball player who once lived the good life until a scandal ruined his career. At a tournament, Lonnie is faced with a possible serious scandal of his own and has to make a difficult decision. This easy-to-read book is filled with action and suspense as you learn about the players and how they play the game and their lives.

There are hundreds of categories and themes and literally hundreds of books I could talk to you about, but this book would be too long! Read through my descriptions and head to the web site I suggested, to your local bookstore, or school library. Take a friend. Read a book together so you can talk about it. Remember, I only included books that my students swear are the best! Some of the books have now become my favorites too.

REFLECT ON WHAT YOU HAVE LEARNED!

What will you do next time when you are looking for a good book to read? What tools will you take with you?

List three books mentioned in this chapter that sound so interesting that you must check them out.

BRAIN TICKLERS
Set # 9

When you answer the following questions, remember to use the strategies discussed in Chapter Two on how to answer multiple-choice questions.

1. Who is the best source for helping you in finding a good book to read?
   a. Your grandparents
   b. Your teachers
   c. Your neighbor
   d. Your friends

2. When browsing for a book, remember to first
   a. Look in a section you are interested in like biographies or fantasy.
   b. Read the last page to find out what happens.
   c. Read the reviews written by the experts.
   d. Look at the cover to see if there is any interesting art work.

3. One of the benefits of using the Internet to find good books is that
   a. You can find out how hard the book is.
   b. You can read reviews written by other teens.
   c. You can see the art work in the book.
   d. You can find out what parents think of the book.

(Answers are on page 191.)

BRAIN TICKLERS—THE ANSWERS

Set # 9, page 190

1. **d.** Remember your friends like the same things as you so they will probably enjoy reading the same books as you too!

2. **a.** Browsing in a large library or bookstore can be overwhelming. You can narrow your choices and browse more easily if you look in a particular section first.

3. **b.** Who better to judge books for teens than teens!

CHAPTER NINE

Further Reading for Teachers and Parents

WHY DO TEENS STRUGGLE WITH READING ANYWAY?

That is a difficult question with more answers than I have room for in this book. We assume students know some reading basics, like the alphabet and phonic sounds, before they enter school. We assume that they learn how to read by the end of first grade. We assume then that they are competent readers by the time they get to junior high school. Assumptions are dangerous.

For example, people assume that those of us who teach junior high and high school English know how to teach reading, and we don't. We are trained to teach students how to analyze text but not how to read it. The assumption, again, is that elementary teachers know how to do that. Of course, elementary teachers are trained how to teach reading, but they may not be well trained to deal with the multiple reading problems students have. The assumption, again, is that children will enter school with some basic skills. But, if a student was not exposed to reading at home or surrounded by literate activities, then he or she may enter school at a disadvantage. Once behind, it is difficult to catch up. So, you see the vicious cycle that students with reading problems are caught up in.

Yes, there are programs in place for those students whose skills are poor. But for those students whose skills are not bad enough, they may not get the help they need. And, for some students, their problems don't develop until they are in junior high or middle school.

Think about it. Elementary students stay with primarily one teacher a day. That teacher surrounds his or her elementary students with wonderful picture story books. Elementary students sit in circles on the floor and are read to. Teachers share stories and images and ask students what they think. And, then—BAM! We ask students to move from classroom to classroom, give them five or more subject-specific books that are several hundred pages long, assign them random and disconnected homework, ask them to join teams and clubs and go to social events, and tell them to write their thoughts instead of verbalizing them. Students go from short chapter-style textbooks to large, informative anthologies and from picture books to novels with no images and pages and pages of words. It's overwhelming. If you think back to your personal experiences, I am sure you too will recall how overwhelming it was for you. For example, write down three positive memories you have about reading and writing in your grades K through 12 school experience. Now, write three negative memories.

Some students make the transition, but some do not. Students may have had no problem with reading until they were asked to manage their time and manage longer and more formal text. It is critical that we provide students at the middle level with a new repertoire of skills. We need to provide them with a toolbox and help them fill it with organizational tools that they can use to build a successful personal reading program for themselves.

In this book, I asked students to first analyze their personal reading strengths and weaknesses and then provided them with user friendly tools that they can use at any point in the reading process. This book is meant to be used either in isolation as a reference tool for an individual student or as a teaching tool in the classroom or at home with a parent. Modeling is key in the reading process, which is why I provided a number of student models. But, I encourage you, the parent and teacher, to model for the student as well. We should never ask students to do something we haven't tried ourselves. Model the reading strategy, guide them through it, and reflect with them on how well that tool worked.

IMPROVEMENT STRATEGIES

The best way to improve a student's reading skills is to have them read. It is imperative that students dive in and practice reading all kinds of text. Just as we need to eat a balanced diet to remain healthy, students need to read a balanced diet of books and materials. They can't read textbooks all the time. Given a choice, I doubt that any of us would voluntarily choose

to read a textbook. Use young adult literature and children's picture books to entice kids into reading. In Chapter Eight, I listed some wonderful books. If you have a student who is struggling with reading but loves comic books, hand that student a graphic novel to read. If you have a student who loves nonfiction, reading about sports figures or celebrities, hand that student a magazine or a biography. If a student's reading skills are so poor that he or she can't handle the textbook or a novel, then a picture book should help the student along because picture books use imagery to help make sense of the text. Meet students where they are and lead them to where you want them to be. Build upon students' interests. Don't assume they know how to help themselves and don't expect them to make the transition to more advanced reading without help. Get them reading something, anything. Once they are reading, have them practice some of the reading strategies in this book.

Balance students' reading instruction. Surround students with a variety of reading materials. Use the textbook, a book of their choice, and an online source. Students need to have some choice in what they read. In the "real" world, those of us who are readers balance our reading. We must read some things that may not be our choice but we also read our favorite morning newspaper, magazine, or best-selling book. If we want our students to be lifelong readers, which should be our ultimate goal, then we need to allow them to function like real readers do. Students must hear highly literate language. Read to them. Read a fiction book, part of a chapter of a textbook, a newspaper article—anything. It can be connected to the curriculum, but that is not necessary. Read for five minutes or the whole period. Encourage students to browse. Ask them what they think. Allow them to talk to other students about what they are reading. In the real world, we browse online and in bookstores and in libraries, we choose our reading materials, and we talk to our friends and families about what we are reading. We must translate those real-world experiences to our students.

Reading improves thinking, and reading improves writing. Every time a student reads, he or she adds new words to his or her brain's word bank. Those additional words allow for more complex thought, and with more words available, for easier and improved writing as well. Remember that we are motivated to learn, and we consider ourselves readers. Our students may not be either. In order for them to make better grades, see improvement on tests, and successfully move to the next grade, we first need to convince them that they can read and that they are readers. We must break it down for them and show them how to conquer difficult text. We must lead them to good reading material. Will this take more time? Yes. Will this make planning lessons or our time schedules more difficult? Yes. Will this make covering the curriculum or completing all homework more difficult? Yes. **BUT**, will we see improvements in our student's attitudes? Yes. Will we see improvement in our student's work? Yes. Will we be creating independent, lifelong readers and learners? Yes. Teaching and parenting is a calling. I encourage you to step up and take the challenge with your student or students.

Get personal! Share your own reading process

The first thing you should do is to get personal with your student or students. Answer the questions in Chapter One. Share your thoughts with them as they share theirs with you. Describe what you like to read and don't like to read. Explain to them how you read text that is boring or hard. For example, do you write in the margins? What do you write? What kinds of conversations do you have with text? Do you underline or highlight? What do you choose to underline or highlight? Do you reread? Why? When you don't understand what you are reading, how do you fix it? Do you make outlines? How do you create an outline? Do you take notes? How do you take your notes? When you need to concentrate, under what environmental conditions do you read? When you are very busy and have a lot of reading to do, how do you manage your time?

The truth is that we have had a lifetime to figure out our tool-box. We learned tricks along the way to make reading easier for us. We watched someone else or were shown how to do something, and we used the things that worked for us. I remember the first time I could use a highlighter in my books because I owned them. That seemed so major at the time. I felt like a real student, but I ran into a problem. Because I had never used a highlighter before, I highlighted everything. After I did poorly on a test, a friend showed me how she highlighted key points and then took notes in her own words in the margin. I started doing that instead and found studying for tests easier because I was rereading a blend of the book's words and my own.

The reading process isn't privileged information. Sharing with students allows them to see that you too have had some struggles, that it's normal, and that you are willing to work with them through this problem. We are all learning as we go. Providing many tools and allowing students to use the ones that work for them will allow them to become independent. The first time I used sticky notes was with a journal article on the Holocaust. I required my students to use all the prompts at least one time. The next time I used sticky notes, I asked my students to have at least five sticky notes in a book chapter and I didn't care which prompts they used. And the next time, I told them it was their choice to use sticky notes. Ninety-five percent of my students used the sticky notes voluntarily the remainder of the year. They liked them because they were fun—something different than just turning the page. They also realized that using sticky notes helped them to maintain their attention. As a result, they realized they had something to contribute to group discussions, and they learned that doing the assignments later was easier. Students also picked up on the vocabulary staircase; many of my students use that tool voluntarily to study for vocabulary tests. They liked having a format with which to study.

A Click Away: Web Sites That Can Help

The good news is that there are too many web sites for reading strategies and graphic organizers. So at press time, I am going to list my favorite sources for both teachers and parents. I used these with my own junior high and high school struggling reader students and now use them with my teacher education students at the university. The sites listed below provide strategies and graphic organizers that can be used for reading practice in any content area. You can find even more web sites by typing in specific search terms such as "reading comprehension strategies," "instructional strategies," or "graphic organizers" into the search engine Google.

- **All About Adolescent Literacy**
  www.adlit.org/
  This site provides bilingual resources for parents and teachers of students in grades 4–12. The resources are rich and diverse and include classroom strategies, PDF graphic organizers that can be used online or in print, current research on hot topics in reading instruction, and a glossary of terms so parents can better understand their child's reading styles and programming.
- **Choice Literacy**
  www.choiceliteracy.com/public/144.cfm
  This site created by literacy leaders for literacy leaders includes reading comprehension strategies and resources by topic and by grade. It even includes podcasts and videos that teachers and parents can use as a model with their own student or students.

- **Glossary of Instructional Strategies**
  www.beesburg.com/edtools/glossary.html
  At press time, this site offered 1,271 different instructional reading, thinking, and writing strategies listed alphabetically from "A, B, C Summarize" to "Zoom in Zoom Out." Each strategy comes with a description and for most even includes additional links and resources that can be used or adapted for use in the classroom or at home.
- **Kathy Schrock's Guide to Everything**
  www.schrockguide.net/concept-mapping.html
  Discovery educator Kathy Schrock has been compiling the best resources for educators for many years now. At this site, scroll down to find graphic organizers and online apps and digital literacy tools that promote critical thinking, reading, and writing opportunities.
- **Reading Quest**
  www.readingquest.org
  Originally, this site was designed to provide social studies teachers with strategies for reading across the curriculum that they could use in their classroom, but the site has become very popular among all educators now, even those in higher education. It provides explanations of reading to learn strategies as well as printable exercises that can be easily understood and modified, leading to successful implementation.

Form a study group: good professional reads

As we guide our students' learning and reading processes and we ask them to eventually become independent and be in charge of their own learning, we should take our own advice. If you want to know more about the reading process and the reading, thinking, and writing connection, then form an informal study group. In fact, if you are an educator, many states will give you license credit or professional renewal hours for taking part in a study group.

Ask fellow teaching colleagues or parents if they are interested in socializing, reading, and talking. With your group, create a list of student needs. Choose books that will help you meet those student needs. Meet a day and time that is convenient for all. Make it fun—bring food, switch locations, and even create themes for each gathering such as chomp and chat! Study groups should be small (between five and eight individuals) so that each member's concerns can be addressed in a timely fashion. Start on time and end on time and meet for only forty-five minutes to one hour. Have a study group leader who says, "Let's get started!" Share the role of study group leader. The leader should create the agenda and that role should change with each meeting. Have a set of study group expectations so the reading is discussed and complaining about current students, schools, administration, and parents is not. Require the teacher to practice new methods for meeting student learning goals. Take the methods and ideas you read and discuss and model, invent, and evaluate practices that have the potential to meet the needs of your students.

Listed below are my five top reads for improving reading comprehension for secondary students. These books are founded in research but are balanced with practical applications. They can be used by a parent or teacher study group.

- *I Read It, but I Don't Get It: Comprehension Strategies for Adolescent Readers* by Cris Tovani is a short, plain-spoken, and accessible book about the reading problems secondary students encounter and how to remedy those problems. This book is actually what inspired me to write my own book. Unlike all the other literacy books I have read, Tovani really understands the real-world struggles of the secondary reader and offers easy and life changing strategies. You will notice that I used many ideas from Tovani's book in Chapter Three of this book. I recommend this book and have witnessed its successful use in many teacher study groups. I encourage all groups to start out with this book.
- *Strategies That Work: Teaching Comprehension to Enhance Understanding* by Stephanie Harvey and Anne Goudvis is really an extension of Tovani's book. It draws upon Tovani's premise and strategies and uses close to forty strategies paired with lessons for understanding text. This book is especially useful for teachers of specialized content areas like social studies and math or parents looking for ideas to help their student with non-English courses. There are also examples of student work, scripts of student dialogue, and lists of good books to pair with lessons.

- *When Kids Can't Read: What Teachers Can Do: A Guide for Teachers 6–12* by Kylene Beers is a book written from the heart. Kylene Beers shares her experiences and epiphanies as a former middle school teacher who discovered that her students couldn't read. She illustrates reading strategies and shows how to make the reading–writing connection. She has catchy phrases for her strategies such as "Say Something," which would appeal to a secondary student reader.

- *Real Reading, Real Writing: Content-Area Strategies* by Donna Hooker Topping and Roberta Ann McManus is a book written by a middle school science teacher and a middle school English teacher. It's a collaboration that showcases real middle school lessons in both English and science and pairs those lessons with reading and writing strategies that work in helping to bring students closer to understanding text. I actually use this as a textbook with a course I teach on reading in the content area. It shares student models and many graphic organizers.

Learning and teaching

Tony Buzan says that "learning to learn is life's most important skill." As well, Oliver Wendell Holmes says that "To teach is to learn again." I encourage you to learn with your students as you share with them the strategies in this book. I ask you to open the door of reading to them. I challenge you to make a difference.

REFLECT ON WHAT I HAVE LEARNED!

That's right! Teachers and parents have to reflect, too. Don't worry, I won't make you take the Brain Ticklers! But, let's turn this information into action!

What are three strategies from this book that you would like to try or implement with your student or students?

What one idea discussed in this chapter resonates with you, made an impact on you?

What is one book from the list of books for improving reading comprehension that you would like to read?

Which web site will you explore first for resources?

WORKS CITED

CHAPTER ONE
[1] Kylene Beers and Barbara G. Samuels, eds. *Into Focus: Understanding and Creating Middle School Readers.* (Norwood, Massachusetts: Christopher Gordon Publishers, Inc., 1998), p. 45.

CHAPTER TWO
[2] Richard T. Vacca and Jo Anne Vacca, *Content Area Reading: Literacy and Learning Across the Curriculum.* (Boston, Massachusetts: Allyn and Bacon, 2002), pp. 203–206.
[3] Jennifer Jacobson and Dottie Raymer, *The Big Book of Reproducible Graphic Organizers (Grades K–8).* (New York: Scholastic, 1999), p. 4.

CHAPTER THREE
[4] Cris Tovani, *I Read It, but I Don't Get It: Comprehension Strategies for Adolescent Readers.* (Portland, Maine: Stenhouse Publishers, 2000), pp. 37–38.
[5] Ibid., p. 38.
[6] Ibid., pp. 101–102.
[7] Ibid., p. 125.

CHAPTER FOUR
[8] "Decipher," *Dictionary.com (http://www.dictionary.com),* October 2, 2003.

CHAPTER FIVE
[9] Tovani, *I Read It, but I Don't Get It: Comprehension Strategies for Adolescent Readers,* pp. 29, 115–118.

CHAPTER SIX
[10] Francis Pleasant Robinson, "SQ3R" *Effective Study, 4th ed.* (New York: Harper and Row, 1970), pp. 32–35.
[11] Tovani, *I Read It, but I Don't Get It: Comprehension Strategies for Adolescent Readers,* pp. 101–102.

CHAPTER SEVEN
[12] Shoup, Barbara. "Building a Rainbow." Barbara Shoup Blog Spot. (*http://www.barbarashoup.blogspot.com/*), June 12, 2011.

INDEX

NOTES

NOTES

Really. This isn't going to hurt at all . . .

Learning won't hurt when middle school and high school students open any *Painless* title. These books transform subjects into fun—emphasizing a touch of humor and entertaining brain-tickler puzzles that are fun to solve.

Bonus Online Component—each title followed by (*) includes additional online games to challenge students, including Beat the Clock, a line match game, and a word scramble.

Each book: Paperback

Painless Algebra, 4th Ed.*
Lynette Long, Ph.D.
ISBN 978-1-4380-0775-5, $9.99, Can$11.99

Painless American Government
Jeffrey Strausser
ISBN 978-0-7641-2601-7, $9.99, Can$11.99

Painless American History, 2nd Ed.
Curt Lader
ISBN 978-0-7641-4231-4, $9.99, Can$11.99

Painless Chemistry
Loris Chen
ISBN 978-0-7641-4602-2, $9.99, Can$11.99

Painless Earth Science
Edward J. Denecke, Jr.
ISBN 978-0-7641-4601-5, $9.99, Can$11.99

Painless English for Speakers of Other Languages, 2nd Ed.
Jeffrey Strausser and José Paniza
ISBN 978-1-4380-0002-2, $9.99, Can$11.50

Painless Fractions, 3rd Ed.
Alyece Cummings, M.A.
ISBN 978-1-4380-0000-8, $9.99, Can$11.50

Painless French, 2nd Ed.
Carol Chaitkin, M.S., and Lynn Gore, M.A.
ISBN 978-0-7641-4762-3, $9.99, Can$11.50

Painless Geometry, 2nd Ed.
Lynette Long, Ph.D.
ISBN 978-0-7641-4230-7, $9.99, Can$11.99

Painless Grammar, 4th Ed.*
Rebecca Elliott, Ph.D.
ISBN 978-1-4380-0774-8, $9.99, Can$11.99

Painless Italian, 2nd Ed.
Marcel Danesi, Ph.D.
ISBN 978-0-7641-4761-6, $9.99, Can$11.50

Painless Math Word Problems, 2nd Ed.
Marcie Abramson, B.S., Ed.M.
ISBN 978-0-7641-4335-9, $9.99, Can$11.99

Painless Poetry, 2nd Ed.
Mary Elizabeth
ISBN 978-0-7641-4591-9, $9.99, Can$11.99

Painless Pre-Algebra, 2nd Ed.*
Amy Stahl
ISBN 978-1-4380-0773-1, $9.99, Can$11.99

Painless Reading Comprehension, 3rd Ed.*
Darolyn "Lyn" Jones, Ed.D.
ISBN 978-1-4380-0769-4, $9.99, Can$11.99

Painless Spanish, 2nd Ed.*
Carlos B. Vega
ISBN 978-0-7641-4711-1, $9.99, Can$11.99

Painless Speaking, 2nd Ed.
Mary Elizabeth
ISBN 978-1-4380-0003-9, $9.99, Can$11.50

Painless Spelling, 3rd Ed.*
Mary Elizabeth
ISBN 978-0-7641-4713-5, $9.99, Can$11.99

Painless Study Techniques
Michael Greenberg
ISBN 978-0-7641-4059-4, $9.99, Can$11.99

Painless Vocabulary, 2nd Ed.*
Michael Greenberg
ISBN 978-0-7641-4714-2, $9.99, Can$11.99

Painless Writing, 3rd Ed.*
Jeffrey Strausser
ISBN 978-1-4380-0784-7, $9.99, Can$11.99

Prices subject to change without notice.

Available at your local book store or visit www.barronseduc.com

Barron's Educational Series, Inc.
250 Wireless Blvd.
Hauppauge, N.Y. 11788
Order toll-free:
1-800-645-3476

(#79) R1/16

ASPIRE HIGHER WITH THE POWER... OF WORDS!

504 ABSOLUTELY ESSENTIAL WORDS, 6th Edition
Builds practical vocabulary skills through funny stories and cartoons plus practice exercises.
ISBN 978-0-7641-4781-4, $12.99, Can$14.99

601 WORDS YOU NEED TO KNOW TO PASS YOUR EXAM, 5th Edition
This new edition hones students' English language skills with 40 updated lessons that include definitions, pronunciation notes, and more. A new section called "Panorama of Words" shows how some of the 601 words are used in a variety of resources, from newspapers to speeches.
ISBN 978-1-4380-0169-2, $14.99, Can$17.99

1100 WORDS YOU NEED TO KNOW, 6th Edition
This book is the way to master more than 1100 useful words and idioms taken from the mass media.
ISBN 978-1-4380-0166-1, $13.99, Can$15.99

AMERICAN SLANG DICTIONARY AND THESAURUS
This unique reference volume is two books in one: an A-to-Z slang dictionary and a slang thesaurus. Words are coded with symbols to help readers distinguish between objectionable and milder slang, and all synonyms are coded for their level of formality.
ISBN 978-0-7641-3861-4, $14.99, Can$17.99

A DICTIONARY OF AMERICAN IDIOMS, 5th Edition
Over 8,000 idiomatic words, expressions, regionalisms, and informal English expressions are defined and cross-referenced for easy access.
ISBN 978-1-4380-0157-9, $16.99, Can$19.50

HANDBOOK OF COMMONLY USED AMERICAN IDIOMS, 5th Edition
With 2500 popular idioms, this book will benefit both English-speaking people and those learning English as a second language.
ISBN 978-1-4380-0167-8, $8.99, Can$9.99

Available at your local book store
or visit www.barronseduc.com

BARRON'S EDUCATIONAL SERIES, INC.
250 Wireless Blvd.
Hauppauge, N.Y. 11788
Order toll-free: 1-800-645-3476
Order by fax: 1-631-434-3217

Prices subject to change without notice.

In Canada:
Georgetown Book Warehouse
34 Armstrong Ave.
Georgetown, Ontario L7G 4R9
Canadian orders: 1-800-247-7160
Order by fax: 1-800-887-1594

(#14) R 11/15

TWO BOOKS IN ONE!

BARRON'S DICTIONARY & THESAURUS

Robert Allen, Editor

Here's an especially handy two-in-one reference volume. The top half of every page serves as a standard dictionary, while the bottom half is a thesaurus that presents selected words from the dictionary section and gives a list of synonyms for each. This dictionary-thesaurus combination offers definitions of more than 40,000 words and phrases, augmented with over 100,000 synonyms. Headwords in both sections are printed in color. Each dictionary headword is designated by its part-of-speech and comes with one or more definitions. Every thesaurus headword—in addition to its list of synonyms—comes with an example sentence that uses the word in context. Corresponding dictionary and thesaurus entries are always cited on the same page for fast, easy reference.

Paperback, 784 pages, 5 1/8" x 7 3/4"
ISBN 978-0-7641-3606-1,
$14.99, Can$17.99

BARRON'S
REFERENCE GUIDES

Dictionary
&
Thesaurus

THE DICTIONARY: More than 40,000 words defined
THE THESAURUS: More than 100,000 synonyms

- All headwords printed in color
- Corresponding dictionary and thesaurus entries on the same page for easy reference

Robert Allen, Editor

***ALSO AVAILABLE IN POCKET SIZE—
SO STUDENTS CAN TAKE IT WHEREVER THEY GO!***

BARRON'S POCKET DICTIONARY & THESAURUS

This pocket-sized edition of the popular larger-format *Barron's Dictionary & Thesaurus* packs more than 40,000 words with their definitions and synonyms into a handy pocket-sized book. It contains all of the same great features that are in the full-size version listed above; however, the new edition is small enough so that students can conveniently fit it into a backpack, carry it to classes, and use it as a reliable reference when writing essays and term papers.

BARRON'S
REFERENCE GUIDES

Pocket
Dictionary
&
Thesaurus

THE DICTIONARY: More than 40,000 words defined
THE THESAURUS: More than 100,000 synonyms

- All headwords printed in color
- Corresponding dictionary and thesaurus entries on the same page for easy reference

Robert Allen, Editor

Paperback with a clear vinyl cover, 796 pages,
4" x 6 1/8"
ISBN 978-0-7641-4305-2
$8.99, Can$10.99

Prices subject to change without notice.

To order visit www.barronseduc.com or your local book store

**Barron's Educational
Series, Inc.**
250 Wireless Blvd.
Hauppauge, N.Y. 11788
Order toll-free: 1-800-645-3476

In Canada:
Georgetown Book Warehouse
34 Armstrong Ave.
Georgetown, Ontario L7G 4R9
Canadian orders: 1-800-247-7160

BARRON'S

(#180) R5/10